Defoe Abbott Marx Hardy Melville Montaigne Machiavelli Chesterton Cooper Emerson Joyce Austen Hugo Eliot Grimm
Stoker Carroll Christie Haggard Molière Schiller
Wilde Maupassant Byron
Garnett Einstein Fitzgerald Engels Hawthorne Smith Kafka
Goethe Dostoyevsky Hall
Cotton Kipling Doyle Willis
Baum Henry Nietzsche
Leslie Dumas Flaubert Turgenev Balzac
Stockton Vatsyayana Crane
Burroughs Verne
Curtis Tocqueville Whitman Gogol Vinci
Homer Widger Tolstoy Busch
Darwin Thoreau Twain Scott Plato
Potter Freud Zola Lawrence Dickens Harte Hesse
Kant Jowett Stevenson Burton
Andersen Voltaire Cervantes
London Descartes
Poe Aristotle Wells Cooke
Hale James Hastings Irving
Bunner Shakespeare
Richter Dante Chambers da Shaw Benedict Alcott
Doré Swift Chekhov Wodehouse Pushkin
Newton

 tredition®

tredition was established in 2006 by Sandra Latusseck and Soenke Schulz. Based in Hamburg, Germany, tredition offers publishing solutions to authors and publishing houses, combined with world-wide distribution of printed and digital book content. tredition is uniquely positioned to enable authors and publishing houses to create books on their own terms and without conventional manu-facturing risks.

For more information please visit: www.tredition.com

TREDITION CLASSICS

This book is part of the TREDITION CLASSICS series. The creators of this series are united by passion for literature and driven by the intention of making all public domain books available in printed format again - worldwide. Most TREDITION CLASSICS titles have been out of print and off the bookstore shelves for decades. At tredition we believe that a great book never goes out of style and that its value is eternal. Several mostly non-profit literature projects provide content to tredition. To support their good work, tredition donates a portion of the proceeds from each sold copy. As a reader of a TREDITION CLASSICS book, you support our mission to save many of the amazing works of world literature from oblivion. See all available books at www.tredition.com.

Project Gutenberg

The content for this book has been graciously provided by Project Gutenberg. Project Gutenberg is a non-profit organization founded by Michael Hart in 1971 at the University of Illinois. The mission of Project Gutenberg is simple: To encourage the creation and distribution of eBooks. Project Gutenberg is the first and largest collection of public domain eBooks.

Overbeck

J. Beavington Atkinson

Imprint

This book is part of TREDITION CLASSICS

Author: J. Beavington Atkinson
Cover design: Buchgut, Berlin – Germany

Publisher: tredition GmbH, Hamburg - Germany
ISBN: 978-3-8472-1620-9

www.tredition.com
www.tredition.de

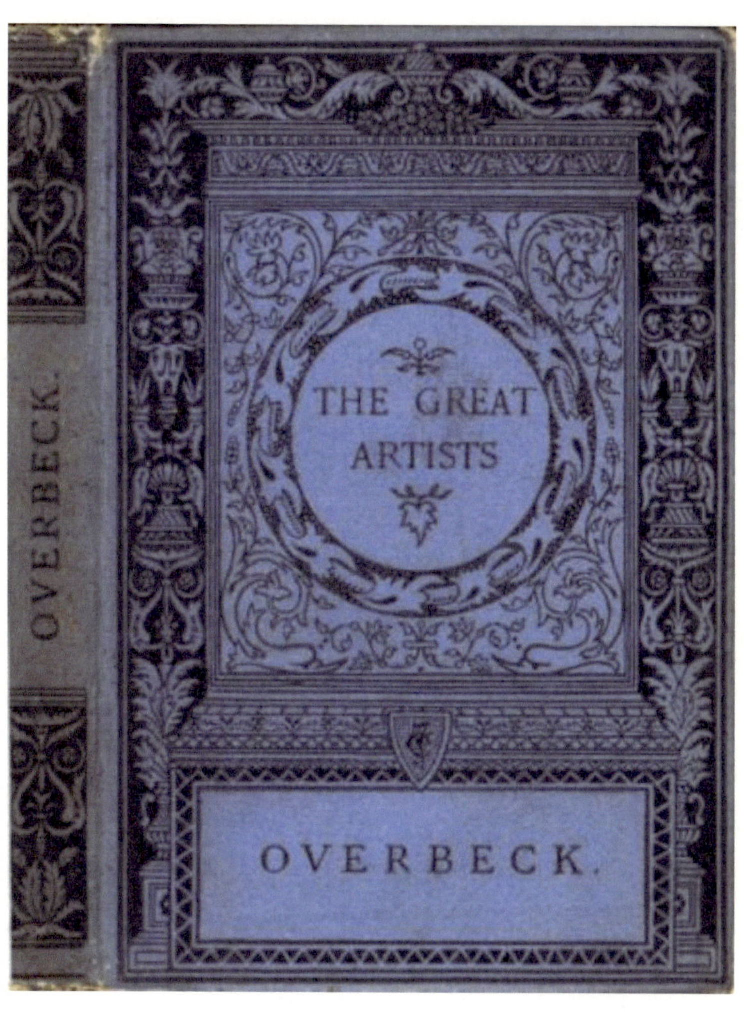

*ILLUSTRATED BIOGRAPHIES OF
THE GREAT ARTISTS.*

JOHANN FRIEDRICH OVERBECK.

ILLUSTRATED BIOGRAPHIES OF THE GREAT ARTISTS.

The following volumes, each illustrated with from 14 to 20 Engravings, are now ready, price 3s. 6d. Those marked with an asterisk are 2s. 6d.

GIOTTO.	By HARRY QUILTER, M.A.
FRA ANGELICO.	By C. M. PHILLIMORE.
FRA BARTOLOMMEO AND ANDREA DEL SARTO.	By LEADER SCOTT.
MANTEGNA AND FRANCIA.	By JULIA CARTWRIGHT.
GHIBERTI AND DONATELLO.*	By LEADER SCOTT.
LUCA DELLA ROBBIA.*	By LEADER SCOTT. *[Nearly ready.*
LEONARDO DA VINCI.	By Dr. J. PAUL RICHTER.
MICHELANGELO BUONARROTI.	By CHARLES CLÉMENT.
RAPHAEL.	By N. D'ANVERS.
TITIAN.	By R. F. HEATH, M.A.
TINTORETTO.	By W. R. OSLER.
CORREGGIO.*	By M. COMPTON HEATON.
VELAZQUEZ.	By E. STOWE, M.A.
MURILLO.*	By ELLEN E. MINOR.
ALBRECHT DÜRER.	By R. F. HEATH, M.A.
THE LITTLE MASTERS OF GERMANY.	By W. B. SCOTT.
HANS HOLBEIN.	By JOSEPH CUNDALL.
OVERBECK.	By J. BEAVINGTON ATKINSON.
REMBRANDT.	By J. W. MOLLETT, B.A.
RUBENS.	By C. W. KETT, M.A.

VAN DYCK AND HALS.	By P. R. HEAD, B.A.	
FIGURE PAINTERS OF HOLLAND.	By LORD RONALD GOWER, F.S.A.	
CLAUDE LORRAIN.*	By OWEN J. DULLEA.	[*In preparation.*
WATTEAU.*	By J. W. MOLLETT, B.A.	[*In preparation.*
VERNET AND DELAROCHE.	By J. RUUTZ REES.	
ROUSSEAU AND MILLET.	By W. E. HENLEY.	[*In preparation.*
MEISSONIER.*	By J. W. MOLLETT, B.A.	
SIR JOSHUA REYNOLDS.	By F. S. PULLING, M.A.	
WILLIAM HOGARTH.	By AUSTIN DOBSON.	
GAINSBOROUGH AND CONSTABLE.	By G. BROCK-ARNOLD, M.A.	
ROMNEY AND LAWRENCE.*	By LORD RONALD GOWER, F.S.A.	
TURNER.	By COSMO MONKHOUSE.	
SIR DAVID WILKIE.	By J. W. MOLLETT, B.A.	
CROME AND THE NORWICH SCHOOL.*	By C. MONKHOUSE.	[*Preparing.*
SIR EDWIN LANDSEER.	By F. G. STEPHENS.	

8

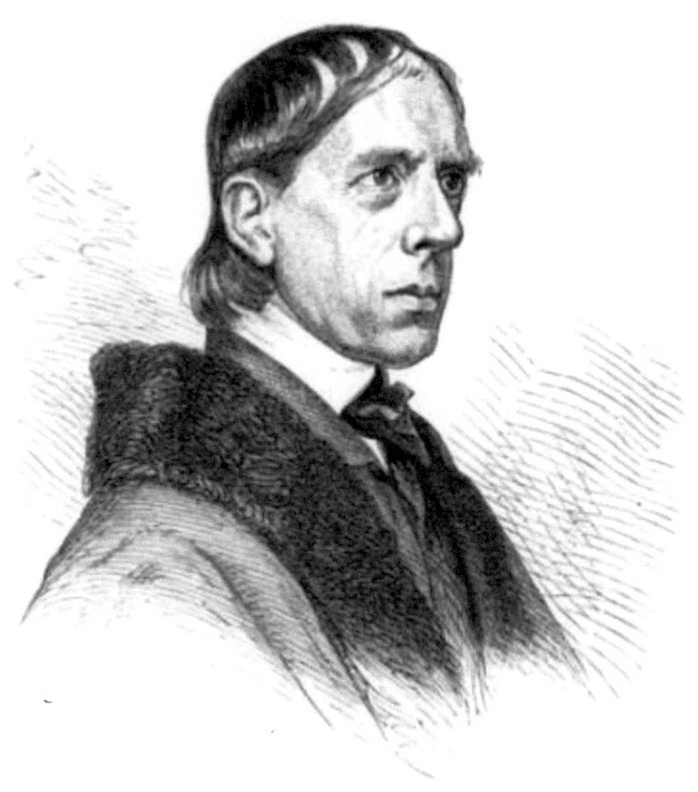

JOHANN FRIEDRICH OVERBECK.

"The whole world without Art would be one great wilderness."

OVERBECK

BY J. BEAVINGTON ATKINSON

AUTHOR OF
'SCHOOLS OF MODERN ART IN GERMANY,'
ETC.

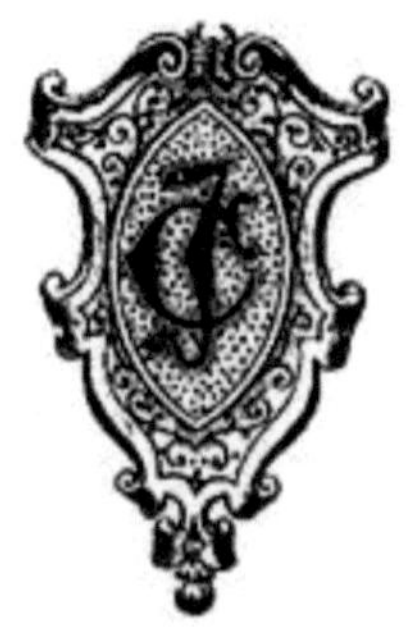

NEW YORK
SCRIBNER AND WELFORD
LONDON
SAMPSON LOW, MARSTON, SEARLE, & RIVINGTON
1882.

TO
THE RIGHT HONOURABLE

A. J. BERESFORD HOPE, ESQ.,

M.P., LL.D.,

THE KIND FRIEND OF ARTISTS,
THE FERVENT UPHOLDER OF CHRISTIAN
ART,

This Life

OF

THE CHRISTIAN PAINTER J. FRIEDRICH OVERBECK

IS

RESPECTFULLY DEDICATED

BY

THE AUTHOR.

PREFACE.

IN offering to the public the first complete biography yet attempted of the painter Overbeck, I wish to give a few words in explanation. The task has been far from easy: the materials, though the reverse of scanty, are scattered: reminiscences of the artist and criticisms on his works lie as fragments dispersed over the current literature of Germany. My endeavour has been to fill in vacuities, to thread together a consistent and connected narrative, and thus, so far as I have been able, to present a true and lucid history.

My duty has been all the more anxious from the unusual complexity of the pictorial products falling under review. The scenes are laid amid the battle of the schools: the periods bring into prominence conflicts between classic, romantic, and naturalistic styles. The art of Overbeck was rooted in the olden times, yet in some degree it became quickened by contact with present life, and took also a personal aspect from the painter's inner self. The great pictures and the numberless drawings thus evolved over a space of more than half a century, and here described from my own knowledge, raise interesting and intricate questions on which the world remains divided. My care has been to give a just estimate of these exceptional art manifestations.

Also enter into the art, through the life, conflicts of religious creeds, strifes between Protestantism and Catholicism, between Platonism, Mysticism, and Rationalism. In dealing with such delicate and serious topics I have avoided all controversy, and have ventured only on the simplest and briefest exposition. My effort has been to state the case fairly all round, to maintain an even balance, and, above all, to place the reader, whatever may chance to be his creed or art school, in a position to form a true judgment.

Likewise fairly to appreciate the artist, it is needful rightly to comprehend the man. And here, again, perplexities arise from unwonted combinations. The character is one of the noblest and purest, and yet it is beset with peculiar infirmities. The portrait offered in these pages is, I trust, true and individual, toned down into unity, and yet not left cold or colourless. Such negation would, indeed, do injustice to my own feelings. For among the cherished recollections of past days are my visits to Overbeck's studio, stretching over a period of twenty years: I learned to revere the master and to love his works, and I trust no word in this little volume may lessen the respect due to an honoured name.

J. B. A.

Kensington,
    May, 1882.

Chart of the Overbeck Family.

CASPAR OVERBECK, Merchant, Religious Refugee. |
CHRISTOPH OVERBECK, Pastor. | CASPAR NIKOLAS
OVERBECK, D. 1752, Pastor. | Total number of Children 8
sons and 6 daughters: 2 sons and 4 daughters died in childhood.

____| __________

__________________________________ | | | | | | | Johann Levin
GEORGE CHRISTIAN OVERBECK, Johann Gottfried August Two Adolph, Conrad, B. 1713, D. 1786, Daniel, Ferdi-
nand, Friedrich, Daughters B. 1706, B. 1712, Doctor of Laws.
B. 1715, B. 1717, B. 1719, who grew to Pastor. Pastor. | D.
1802, Apothecary. School womanhood. | Doctor of Teacher.
| Theology, &c.

________________________| ______________________________

________________ | | | Conrad, CHRISTIAN ADOLPH
OVERBECK, Johann George, Died at Riga, B. 1755, M. 1781,
D. 1821. D. 1819, Merchant. Doctor of Laws, Syndic, Bürger-
meister of Lübeck, &c. Pastor. | 4 sons and 2 daughters: one
son died in childhood.

__________________________________| __________________

____________________ | | | | | Christian Gerhard, Johan-
nes, JOHANN FRIEDRICH OVERBECK, Frau Charlotte Frau
Elizabeth B. 1784, D. 1846, D. 1830, B. in Lübeck 1789, M.
1819, Leithoff, Meyer, Judge, Lübeck. Merchant. D. in Rome
1869 deceased. deceased. | | The Painter | Christian Theo-
dore, | | Frau Harms, B. 1818, D. 1880, | | Lübeck, Doctor,
Senator; | |__________________ living. left no children. | | |

____________________| __________________

____ |________________ | | | | | | Johannes, Gustav, Ar-
nold, Frau Rath ALFONS MARIA, Daughter of the Professor,
Düsseldorf, Düsseldorf, Reuleaux, Son of the Painter, Painter:
died Doctor, living. living. Berlin, B. 1822, D. 1840. in childhood. Archæologist, living. Leipzig, living.

OVERBECK.

CHAPTER I.

LÜBECK — VIENNA.

JOHANN FRIEDRICH OVERBECK was born, as a tablet on his father's house records, in Lübeck on the 4th of July, 1789. Among his ancestors were Doctors of Law and Evangelical Pastors. His parents were good Protestants; his father was Burgomaster in the ancient city. Seldom has a life been so nicely preordained as that of the young religious painter. The light of his coming did not shine, as commonly supposed, out of surrounding darkness. A visit to his birth-place, expressly made for this memoir, soon showed me that Overbeck, from his youth upwards, had been tenderly cared for; that he received a classic education; that his mind was brought under moral and religious discipline; in short, that the rich harvest of later years had found its seed-time here within the family home in Lübeck.

The old house in which Overbeck was born has unfortunately, within the last few years, been modernised, but the original medallion relief of the painter's head, life-size, is built into the new façade, and the former structure can be accurately ascertained as well from the designs of the adjoining tenements as from the living testimony of the neighbours.[1] The Overbeck mansion stood in the König Strasse, a principal thoroughfare in the heart of an old city which may not inaptly be designated the Nuremberg of Northern Germany. It is not difficult here on the spot to picture the life of the painter while yet in his teens. The historic town of Lübeck had enjoyed a signal political, commercial and artistic epoch. As the head of the Hanseatic League, it rose to unexampled prosperity. Deputies from eighty confederate municipalities assembled in the audience-chamber of the Rathhaus; fortifications, walls and gateways were reared for defence, and merchant princes made their opulence and love of ostentation conspicuous in dwellings of imposing and picturesque design; thus pointed gables, high-pitched overhanging roofs, stamp with mediæval character the present streets. Then, too, were founded rich ecclesiastical establishments; then was built the cathedral, containing among other treasures matchless brasses, a unique rood-loft, and a double triptych, the masterpiece of Memling. This sacred work made a deep impression on young Overbeck, and is known to have given a direction to his art. About the same period was also reared the Marien Kirche, enriched with bronze sacrament-house, old German triptychs and fine painted glass. This is the church in which the painter's father,

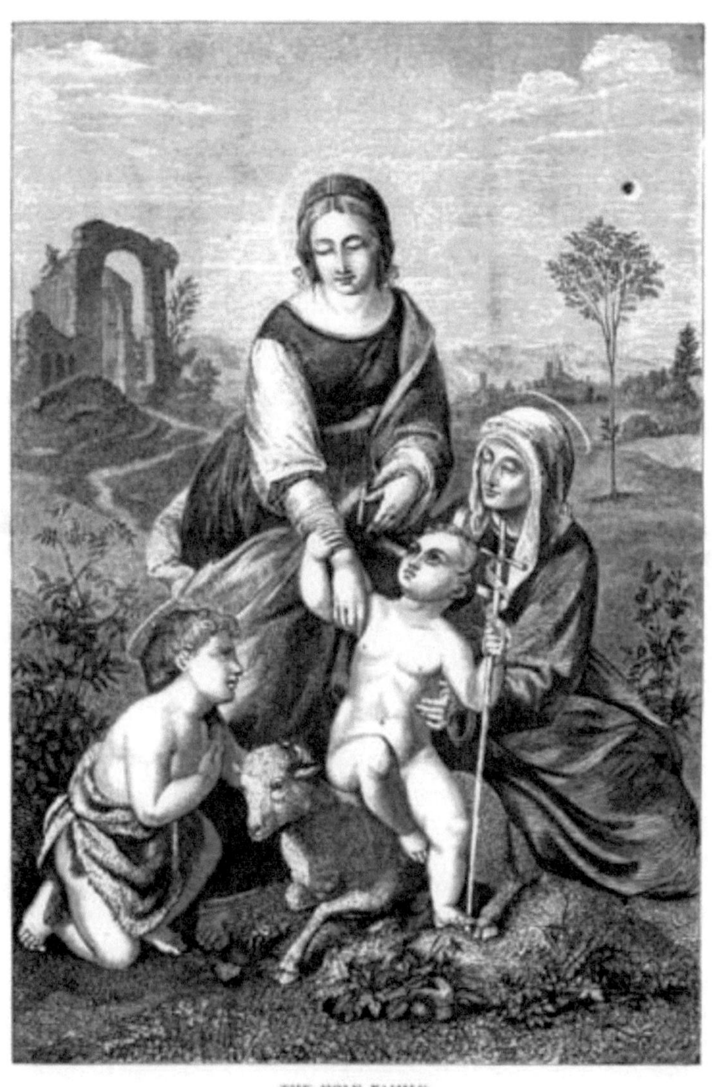

THE HOLY FAMILY.

as Burgomaster, had a distinguished stall, elaborately carved; and now, on visiting the spot, I find appropriately among the treasures two chefs-d'œuvre which the son affectionately wrought for the city of his birth. These churches are Protestant, but fortunately the worst sign of the Reformation is whitewash, and so the relics of the past are reverently conserved, and here in Lübeck, as in Nuremberg, the Madonna still holds her honoured niche, and the saints yet shine from out the painted window, even as in after-years the selfsame characters appeared on the canvases of Overbeck. Amid associations thus sacred, encircled by a family addicted to learning and piety, to poetry and art, was the tranquil spirit of the young painter led into meditative paths; and as I took my evening walk at the setting of the sun by the side of the wooded river, under shadow of the old gateways and churches, it was not very hard to realize how the love of nature and of art grew up in the mind of the young student, and how this city of the past proved a fitting prelude to a noble life-work which set as its goal the revival of what was best and most beautiful in the olden times.

The family of Overbeck had been for generations preeminent for learning and piety, and biographers have scarcely sufficiently taken into account either the Classic or the Christian inheritance of the painter. Religious teaching and living came by long lineal descent (see Family Chart on page xvi.): the great, great, great grandfather, Caspar Overbeck, was a religious refugee; the next in succession, Christoph, was a Protestant pastor; and to the same sacred calling belonged his son, Caspar Nikolas, who lived into the middle of the last century. After comes the grandfather, George Christian, Doctor of Laws; and among collaterals signally shines the great-uncle, Johann Daniel Overbeck (died 1802, aged 88);[2] this memorable man was Doctor of Theology, Rector of the Lübeck Gymnasium, and a voluminous writer; he published thirty or more treatises; among the number are 'The Spirit of Religion,' 'Grounds of Agreement in Religion through the Reason and the Understanding;' also discourses on St. Peter, St. Paul, and Luther. Facility of pen runs through the family. Two other great-uncles, Johann Adolph and Levin Conrad Overbeck, brothers of the Doctor of Theology, were Pastors: furthermore must not be forgotten the uncle, Johann George (brother of the Burgomaster), who lived till 1819, and is described as a faithful untiring pastor to an evangelical congregation, who offered his life a willing sacrifice. "Duty" might be the watch-word of all who bear the name of Overbeck. Lastly, and not least, appears the pious, learned, and æsthetic father, Christian Adolph. Though not in holy orders, he concerned himself variously with religion in the wide and vital sense of the word, holding it a divine presence, the rule of life, and the inspirer of all noble work. I should judge he was not dogmatic in creed, nor rigid in ceremonial. He was philosophic, but had too much heart to be a rationalist; too much imagination for an anti-supernaturalist. He was a mystic pietist; religion blending with poetry coloured his whole mind; revelation, nature, and art, were for him one and indivisible. And this I believe to have been the mental state of the son while yet under the parental roof. The sequel will show a change; the incertitude of speculation could not be sustained, and so anchorage was sought within an "Infallible Church." Yet for the right reading of a character curiously subtle and complex, it is needful to realise the fact that the seeds sown in the homestead were never uprooted, that it was, indeed, the old stock which sustained the new grafting, and that, to the last, a poetic mysticism dwelt in the chambers of the artist's mind. And as was the tree so were the fruits; sprung from a family of preachers, the painter became an evangelist in his art.

The father, Dr. Christian Adolph Overbeck, as the formative type of the son, merits a further word.[3] If not quite a genius, he was the model of a scholar and a gentleman; besides being Burgomaster in the city of his birth, he was Doctor of Laws, Syndic of the Cathedral Chapter, and served in important political missions to Paris and St. Petersburg. He is described "Musis Amicus";[4] and not only the friend of poesy, he was a poet himself, and by virtue of the duality habitual to his mind dedicated his pen with singular impartiality to Christ and Apollo; one volume of verses being entitled 'Anacreon and Sappho,' another, containing a poem, on 'The Love of God.' These products rise somewhat above the level of respectable mediocrity, yet they have not escaped the stigma of platitudes. Goethe, however, did not disdain to make respectful mention of the poet. The painter inherited in some small degree the paternal gift; he accompanied with verses the engraved and published drawings, *Jesus as a Child in the House at Nazareth.* By the father I have also before me a "new edition," published 1831, of a collection entitled 'Frizchens Lieder,'[5] so called because penned for the benefit of the youthful Frederick. The preface makes mention of "my little Frizchen" thus:—"It were better had he been an angel, but he is just a human child:" then, facetiously, it is added, "he is less ideal than saucy and conceited." Those who like myself knew only the solemnity of the painter in advanced years have a difficulty in supposing in the child such traits compatible. These songs of the domestic affections were set to music; the father, as a dilettante complete, cultivated all the harmonies whether of thought, form, or sound; the home was musical.

The family life composes into a placid, homelike picture. The parents, though well to do, were far from affluent. The stipends of the busy Burgomaster and Syndic were small, and he remained comparatively poor. At the age of twenty-six he married a young widow with money and one daughter, and domestic cares necessarily thickened with the birth of six additional children, two daughters and four sons, of whom Frederick was the youngest. The mother, we are told, was beloved and honoured, and in addition to ordinary domestic duties, diligently assisted her children in the preparation of their school lessons; moreover it is expressly stated that her fortune contributed largely to the household expenses. The would-be artist could not be considered unfortunate in his worldly condition; he entered on life removed equally from the extremes of riches or poverty; his parents were sufficiently well off to make it possible for him to gratify his tastes in the choice of a profession, while he was always under such pressure as to render it imperative that he should put out his full powers. His education within the limits of a provincial town was liberal; the father kept himself and his household quiet, student-like, and sequestered from the dissipation of society, and so all the better could be cultivated the budding faculties of his offspring. When the children were sufficiently advanced he joined with other parents in engaging a qualified tutor, and so formed a special class or superior school. With affection was watched the inclination towards art of the youngest son, and anxiety lessened as the faculty strongly declared itself, for above all was dreaded "mediocrity as the deadly sin of artists." The father held that for success in art as a profession three conditions were essential; classic training, nobility of mind, and technical skill. And so in each day the foremost place was assigned to classic studies. As to the formation of character, religion stood as the corner-stone, and the maxim for the daily life was "love in a pure mind." This axiom sounds to me as the key-note to the painter's lifelong art—an art loving in spirit and kept unspotted from the world. But the father and son differed in this—that the one was eclectic, the other exclusive. The father, with the wide toleration of a poet-philosopher, believed in the possibility of harmoniously combining styles, Classic, Romantic, and Christian. His views may be judged from the following:

The Father's Monition to study the Classics.

With joy I see you constant in the study of the ancients. To the Greeks and old Romans was it given to stand as the everlasting lawgivers of the beautiful. Well for you that you read the classics: above all, acquaint yourself with the glorious forerunner, Homer, of whom almost every line is a picture. Homer in the right chamber of the heart, and the Bible in the left—or *vice-versâ*—in this way, it seems to me, you cannot go far astray.

Creed for a Purist Painter.

The artist's and poet's mind should be as a spotless mirror: his heart must be pure and pious, at one with God and all mankind. The path to the holy Temple of Art lies apart from the world, and the painter will go on his way all the more unassailed if he stand aloof from the temptations of the senses. And if the artist's mind be a temple, then should find place therein only the figures of saints and the semblances of holy things; and even in profane representations a heavenly spirit should reign. The mind is raised by the contemplation of the master-works of genius, thus art reaches the highest summit.

It is not to be supposed that the youth while in Lübeck reached the father's ideal; but within a stone's throw of the house lay a Gymnasium, including a Drawing School of which the great uncle, Dr. Johann Daniel Overbeck, had been head master. Here, on the spot, I am told the nephew received from a certain Professor Feder-au instruction in art, and I have before me a drawing, the earliest that has come to my knowledge, which proves that the pupil was at least painstaking. The subject, in accordance with the father's precept, is Homeric, the well-known meeting of Ulysses and Telemachus.[6] After the prevailing manner of the period, the style is classic, according to the French school of David, and a Greek portico appropriately finds a place in the background. Young Overbeck discovered in the sequel how much he had to learn, and to unlearn; he closed Homer to open his Bible.

The time came for a change in the scene of action, the art resources of a small provincial town were exhausted, and the necessity arose for thorough academic training elsewhere. The choice in those days was not extended, and after due consideration the election fell in favour of Vienna. Accordingly, in March, 1806, at the age of seventeen, young Overbeck left Lübeck. The home-parting was tender, and might have been heart-rending could the future have been read. Never were son and parents to meet again. Frederick in sundry years, when full of honours, visited Germany, but he seemed to shrink from a return to the scenes of his youth; change in religion may have made contact painful. Yet we are told that closest communication was kept up by constant correspondence; that the father affectionately watched his son's illustrious career and read with lively satisfaction all announcements in the public journals. The mother died in 1820, the father a year after: for forty years they had been lovingly united. I have visited the retired "God's-acre," beyond the gates, removed from the noisy traffic of the town, and not without difficulty discovered the grave of father and mother. So dense was the overgrowth of years, that not a letter on the massive stone could be seen; but the old man of the place, tearing away the thick mantle of ivy, revealed the words, "Here rest in God Elizabeth Overbeck, and Christian Adolph Overbeck, Burgomaster."

On reaching Vienna, the super-sensuous painter did not find a bed of roses: his tastes were fastidious, his habits exclusive, his aspirations impracticable. Of course his art remained as yet unremunerative; thus his means were scanty, and the friends he might have hoped to make turned out enemies. And it cannot be denied that the state of things in Vienna was enough to discourage and disgust an earnest, truth-seeking student. The Academy into which the Christian artist entered was under the direction of Friedrich Füger, a painter of the French type, not without renown, but given over to the service of Jupiter, Prometheus, and Venus, and when he chanced to turn to sacred subjects, such as *The Death of Abel* and *The Reading Magdalen*, affectation and empty pretence were his resource. I have seldom seen works more contemptible. Overbeck was in despair, and wrote to a friend that he had fallen among a vulgar set, that every better feeling, every noble thought, was suppressed within the Academy, and that, losing all faith in humanity and in art, he turned inwardly on himself. This transcendental strain, I cannot but think, came in some measure from the conceit incident to youth; self-complaisancy was certainly a habit of mind which the painter persistently cultivated as a virtue.

Four years' work within an organised academy could not be otherwise than a gain to a tyro who had everything to learn. Director Füger was at least thoroughly trained; talent and industry had early won him the distinction of pensioner to Rome, and he subsequently executed important frescoes in Naples, which obtain honourable mention in the history of the times. His school might be bad, but still it was a school; and the fact cannot be controverted that Overbeck issued from it an artist. He learnt what his father had laid down as essential to success, drawing, composition, technique, and his advance was such, that while in Vienna he commenced, and in part painted, *Christ's Entry into Jerusalem*, a prized possession to this day in the Marien Kirche, Lübeck. Moreover, I am inclined to think that under Füger he was grounded in the art of wall-painting, not only as a manipulative method, but as a system of composition and decoration; otherwise it is hard to understand how, shortly after arriving in Rome, he knew more about fresco than the Italians themselves. Overbeck and his master, however, became all the more irreconcilable because the discords lay less in the letter than in the spirit.

In order to realise Overbeck's artistic and mental difficulties here in Vienna, and afterwards in Rome, it may be well in fewest words to indicate the perplexed state of things in Germany generally—a wide theme on which volumes have been written. We have to consider that Europe had suffered under the throes of the great French Revolution, and that then followed the galling despotism of Napoleon. Art and literature lay frozen and paralysed, and Overbeck in Lübeck and Vienna, like Cornelius in Düsseldorf, found in tyrannous sway the pseudo-classic school of the French David, cold as marble, rigid as petrifaction, spasmodic as a galvanised muscle. But the Germans, especially the more intellectual sort, smarting under the yoke, were all the while gathering strength to reclaim nationality as their birthright. The reaction came through the romantic movement, otherwise the revival of the poetry and the art of the Middle Ages. Overbeck fell under the influence: in his Lübeck home he read Tieck's 'Phantasies on Art,' and thirsted for the regeneration drawing near. In Rome the spell heightened; thinkers such as Frederick Schlegel brought over proselytes, and the painter's early frescoes from Tasso's 'Jerusalem Delivered,' came as the specific products of the new era. But the School of Romance wore two aspects; the one, Poetic and Chivalrous; the other expressly Christian; and Overbeck was not content to exchange Homer and Virgil for Dante and Tasso, he turned from the age of Pericles and Augustus to the nativity of Christ. And it seemed to him that the pure spring of

Christian Art had, not only in Vienna but throughout Europe, been for long diverted and corrupted, and so he sought out afresh the living source, and casting on one side his contemporaries, took for his guides the pre-Raphaelite masters. Such is the relation in which he stands to the Romantic movement.

But the election made in favour of an art born of Christianity proved for Overbeck the severer conflict, because Germany, in the generation scarcely passed away, had experienced a studious classic revival under the critic Winckelmann and the painters Mengs and Carstens. Goethe, too, a tyrant in power, had thrown his weight into the classic scale, and, much to the chagrin of the young painter, declared that the highest Christian Art was but the perfecting of humanity. Moreover, classicism had been brought within the painter's home by a five years' sojourn in Lübeck of Carstens, the Flaxman of Germany. The father befriended the poor artist, and being well-read in Greek and Roman authors, supplied him, among other needs, with ideas for his classic compositions. I deem these facts should be duly considered; it is wholly false to ignore the presence of a classic element in the Christian Art of Overbeck; and just as the purest religious painters of Italy borrowed from the Pagans, so the great Christian Artist of our times culled from the antique all he could assimilate. It is clear to me, judging from the internal evidence of his works, that as a student Overbeck went through the usual course of drawing from the plaster cast. Many are the passages in his compositions which might be quoted in point, particularly Biblical incidents, such as the *Expulsion from Paradise*, wherein appear undraped figures. Here are seen to advantage the generic form, the typical beauty, the harmony of line, the symmetry, which distinguish the Classic from the Gothic. Furthermore, Overbeck from first to last eschewed the dress actually worn in the Holy Land, and deliberately draped Christ and the Apostles as Greek sages and Roman senators. I believe in so doing he was on the whole wise, his motive being to remove his characters from the sphere of common life; even for him, the most single-minded of men, art was a compromise: but while borrowing thus largely both in figure and costume from the Classic, it were vain to contend that his creations had an exclusively Christian origin. I may add that I do not think the controversy lies so much between religions as between historic

Schools of Art. Overbeck was so much the artist that, like Raphael, he made beauty wherever extant his own, only caring that whatever was taken from the Pagan should be baptized with the Christian spirit. Thus much indeed is confessed in his explanatory text to his master-work the *Triumph of Religion in the Arts*. Therefore in quoting his own words the subject may fairly be allowed to drop: he writes: "Although heathenism, as such, should be looked upon by the Christian painter with decided disdain, yet the arts as well as the literature of the ancients may be turned to advantage, as the children of Israel employed the gold and silver vessels which they brought with them out of Egypt in the service of the true God in His Temple, after melting them down and consecrating them anew."

The much abused Director Füger was the champion, as we have seen, of hybrid classicism, hence the hostility between master and pupil. The precise attitude assumed by the contending parties it is not very easy to define; but that there were faults on both sides may easily be conceded; that each was in extreme is also evident, and that Overbeck was the last man to yield an inch or to meet half way is equally certain. The fatal conflict broke out in differences as to the modes of study: of the Academy we should now say that it was conventional, wedded to false methods, in short, that it had wholly lost the right road in the devious paths of decadence. The young innovators, not choosing to conform, assumed a defiant position analogous to, though not identical with, that taken half a century later by our English pre-Raphaelite brethren. The study of the early masters in the royal collection they preferred to the routine of the Academy; thus Dürer and Perugino were held up in challenge to Correggio and Rubens, the idols of the day. Then the discord was equally violent as to the right mode of studying nature. The charge made against the German pre-Raphaelite Brotherhood was that they dealt with the life-model crudely and inartistically; on the contrary, Overbeck and his adherents declared that they sought for nothing else than truth, only they held that nature should not be studied superficially, but with the end of deciphering her hidden meanings. The human body they looked on as a temple, the face they read as the mirror of the mind. All this, and much more besides, though then a novelty, is now an old story; the doctrine that the bodily form is moulded on the spiritual being, the speculations concerning the relations between the "objective" and the "subjective," the outward and the inward, the correspondence between the world of sense and the world of thought, have one and all taken definite place in the history of mental philosophy. We have here fully to realise that Overbeck had breathed the atmosphere of mystic spiritualism in Lübeck; hence his entrance into "spiritual art," hence his "soul pictures." His mind being thus sublimated, he looked down upon the Viennese Academicians as common and unclean; a rupture naturally ensued, and he and his companions being in the minority, were with a strong hand, and with little ceremony, expelled from the classes. The blow for the moment seemed overwhelming, yet it brought salvation. Had Overbeck remained chained to the Academy, art through him would not have seen a new birth. His course became clear: he quitted Vienna for Rome, the city of his desire.

In the fourth and last year of the painter's apprenticeship in the Austrian capital, was begun a really arduous composition, *Christ's Entry into Jerusalem*.[7] The picture is of the utmost import as affording the only evidence of the artist's attainments in Vienna. In the first place to be remarked is the striking fact that not a vestige remains of the French school of David, or of the showy masters of the Italian decadence; the work, indeed, might have been designed as a protest against the Viennese Academy, and as a justification of the painter's revolt. The style adopted is conjointly that of the Italian pre-Raphaelite and of the early German and Flemish masters. The background is built up into a high horizon giving support to the foreground figures; the colours are deep and lustrous, and so far contrast favourably with the weaker and cruder tones unfortunately adopted at a later period. The costume is a deliberate compromise between the classic and the naturalistic. Nowhere does the artist venture, as Horace Vernet, on the Bedouin dress. Christ is clothed in a flowing robe, while the Apostles, as in the compositions of Raphael, belong less to the Holy Land than to the Roman Forum. This treatment of draperies was adhered to through all subsequent works, the only change being further generalisation and a wider departure from naturalism. In fact it is curious to observe in this early work how much nature enters; figures and incidents come direct from life, as witness portraits of contemporaries, groups of little children, young mothers and aged women. Such passages are happily destitute of what the Viennese academicians called "style;" they have more of the old German angularity than of "the Grecian bend." Yet always with Overbeck Beauty is present, only not thrust in, as by the academicians of the period, in violation of Truth and Goodness. Also very noteworthy is the impress of thought in the heads, hands, and attitudes; the painter, as we have seen, came of a family of thinkers, and the purport of his art was to give expression to mind. Here again he took as his teachers the early masters, so that these figures, though more or less studied from nature, might seem to have walked out from an old panel picture, yet they are more than complications, they are impressed with the painter's own individuality. Altogether the work marks not only a starting-point in Overbeck's life, but a new era in the art of the nineteenth century.

The composition by lapse of time gains biographic and historic value through the introduction, in accordance with the practice of the old masters, of contemporary portraits. The painter has placed among the spectators his father, in character of Burgomaster, also close by, his mother, a remarkably shrewd old lady. His wife, memorable as a beauty, is grouped with the three Marys, and by her side sports the painter's much-loved son, a boy, palm-branch in hand, rejoicing with the multitude. Nor are the pilgrim painters in Rome forgotten: Overbeck and his brother artists, Cornelius and others, appear at respectful distance, gazing on Christ riding into Jerusalem.

Overbeck, before quitting Vienna, pretty much determined his vocation: he resolved to dedicate his life to Christian Art. On the point of departure, in writing to a friend in Lübeck, he takes a retrospective view, and also points to the future. He recalls evening walks under the shade of trees with congenial companions; he remembers earnest conversations on poetry, painting, and other manifestations of the beautiful, yet still something remained wanting. True art, he writes, he had sought in vain: "Oh, I was so full of it, my whole fancy was possessed by Madonnas and Christs; I bore these impressions about with me, I cherished them, but nowhere could I find response." In Vienna, as we have seen, the desire of his soul remained unsatisfied. His conflicts were painful, but once for all he declares, "I will abide by the Bible; I elect it as my standing-point." A few friends were like-minded, and one especially, who had come from Italy, encouraged a pilgrimage to the land of Christian Art. Accordingly, Overbeck packed up his small worldly possessions, of which the canvas of *Christ's Entry into Jerusalem* was the most considerable, and at length he reached Rome as a haven of rest.

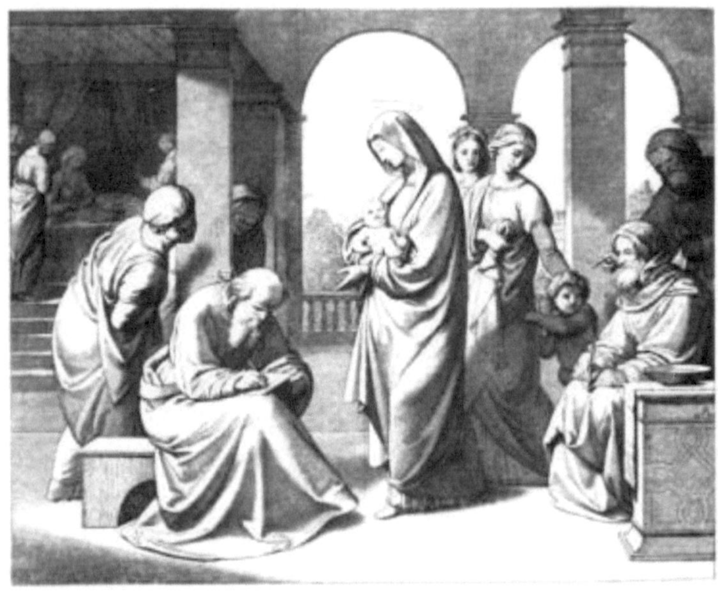

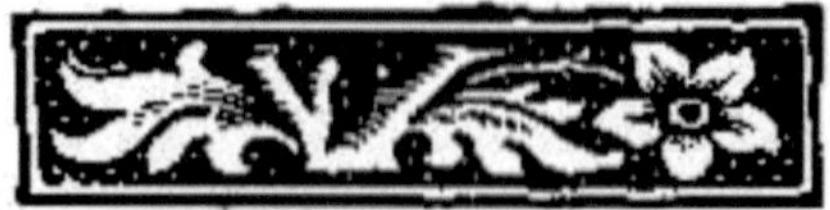

FOOTNOTES:

[1] The Overbeck house, when I sought it out in 1880, was rebuilt and retenanted; the ground floor happens to be now occupied by a

bookseller and fancy stationer, who sustains intact the Protestant character of the establishment. In vain I enquired for engravings from Overbeck; the nearest approach to religious art was a portrait of Luther in chromo-lithography!

[2] See 'Leben Herrn Johann Daniel Overbeck, weiland Doctors der Theologie und Rectors des Lübeckischen Gymnasiums, von einem nahen Verwandten, und vormaligen Schüler des Verewigten.' Lübeck, 1803.

[3] See 'Zur Erinnerung an Christian Adolph Overbeck, beider Rechte Doctor und Bürgermeister zu Lübeck.' Lübeck, 1830.

[4] I have seen in the Public Library, Lübeck, the engraved portrait inscribed with the above words; the head bears a striking resemblance to the well-known features of the son: the profile shows a fine intellectual type, the forehead is ample and overhanging, the coronal region full, the eye searching and earnest, the upper lip long, the mouth large and firmly set. The last was not the most beautiful feature in the painter's remarkable face.

[5] 'Frizchens Lieder, herausgegeben von Christian Adolph Overbeck: neue Ausgabe.' Hamburg, Verlag von August Campe, 1831.

[6] This juvenile exercise, probably only a copy, was given by young Overbeck to his master, and is now in the Town Library; it is washed in with Indian ink, measures two feet by one foot nine inches, and is signed and dated "F. Overbeck, 1805-21 April." The Gymnasium, like the House, has recently been rebuilt, but the continuity of learning remains unbroken—boys flock to the school as in the painter's youth. The adjoining Town Library also contains the original cartoon, drawn in Rome, for one of the frescoes illustrative of Tasso in the Villa Massimo, length about ten feet; likewise the cartoon of the Vision of St. Francis, painted in fresco in Sta. Maria degli Angeli, near Assisi; the cartoon is about twenty feet long, the figures are life-size.

[7] This picture, on canvas, is nearly eight feet long by six feet high, the figures are about three feet. The 'Lübeckische Blätter' states that "Overbeck began the work in Vienna in 1809, in the fourth year of his art study, and there completed the background and the fig-

ures in the middle plane, and that it was taken by him to Rome in 1810." In the course of time the foreground figures were introduced, but not till 1824 did the picture reach completion. It bears the signature and date "J. F. Overbeck, 1824." Thus fifteen years elapsed between the first touch and the last, and some ten further years passed before the canvas came to the artist's native city. I carefully examined the painting in the Marien Kirche in October, 1880, and found it in perfect preservation, the colours unchanged, the surface untouched by time or restoration. The picture differs from the illustration to these pages.

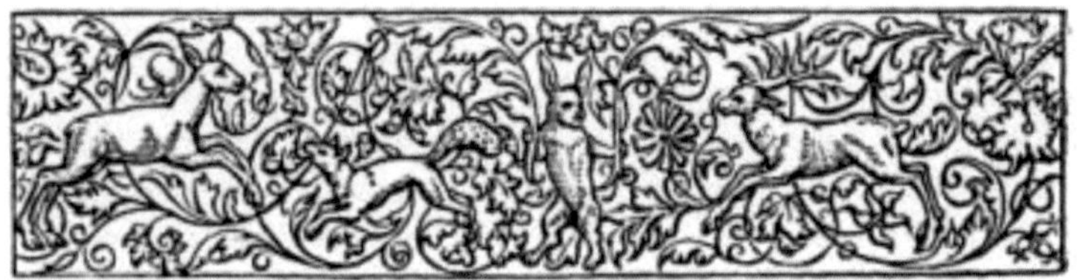

CHAPTER II.

ROME — THE GERMAN BROTHERHOOD.

THE biographies of artists, proverbially picturesque, present few scenes more pleasant to look on than the early years in Rome of the Brotherhood of German Painters, of whom Overbeck and his friend Cornelius were the leaders. Exiles in some sort from their native land, they entered Italy as pilgrims, and were not far from suffering as martyrs. They were devout, hard-working, and withal poor. They had been drawn from distant cities to Rome as a common focus, and there they severed themselves from ignoble present times, and abiding quietly amid ancient monuments and sacred shrines, sought to make the days of old live anew. So congenial did Rome prove to Overbeck, that he could hardly be induced to sever himself from the city or its neighbourhood over a space of more than fifty years. The task he assigned to himself was arduous: how he went to work and accomplished his mission I shall try to show.

Overbeck, in company with his brother artists, Pforr, Vogel and Hottinger, having in Vienna cast off all fetters, entered Rome as freemen in 1810. A year later Cornelius, as a young Hercules, came upon the scene; he had fought his way from Düsseldorf; like Overbeck, he had found the Academy a burden and a snare, and he betook himself to Italy for deliverance. Then began that closest friendship between the two painters which, lasting for more than half a century, was severed only by death. Cornelius, writing to his friend Mosler, describes the German Brotherhood in Rome, and adds: "Overbeck from Lübeck is the one who by the gentleness and nobility of his soul draws all around him; he inspires them to everything true and beautiful. May be he is the greatest artist now living: you would be astonished if you could see him at his work. Yet he is the most humble and retiring of men." If Overbeck were as a lamb, surely Cornelius was a lion, each indeed supplied what was lacking in the other. Cornelius in after years said to Rudolf Lehmann, "I am the man, he is the woman." And it may strike the mind as a singular coincidence, or rather as a benignant disposition of Providence, that at sundry turning-points in the world's history, two men the opposites the one of the other have been conjoined, as if for the better accomplishment of the work to be done. We may recall, in art, Raphael and Michelangelo; in religion, St. John and St. Peter, Melanchthon and Luther; and in philosophy, Plato and Aristotle. At the risk of pushing the analogy too far, it may be added that Cornelius was positive as Aristotle, impetuous as St. Peter and Luther, defiant as Michelangelo; while in contrast, Overbeck shared with Plato idealism, with St. John love, with Melanchthon gentleness, and with Raphael grace.

The German colony of pre-Raphaelite painters in Rome grew, and in after years came accessions almost unintermittingly.[1] Within the first twelve months were gathered together, as we have seen, Overbeck, Cornelius, Pforr, Vogel and Hottinger. Soon followed the brothers Wilhelm and Rudolf Schadow: to these must be added Koch, Wintergerst, Sutter, Mosler, Veit, Schnorr, Eggers, Platner, and others. Later came Joseph Führich, who literally worshipped the ground on which Overbeck stood. Edward Steinle, of a younger generation, was also a bosom friend of the painter. Later still arrived young zealots from Düsseldorf, where Schadow had established the renowned school of religious art. The best known of these disciples are Ernst Deger, Franz Ittenbach, and the brothers Andreas and Carl Müller. After sitting at the feet of Overbeck in Rome, it was their privilege to paint the chapel at Remagen on the Rhine: these frescoes are accepted as among the most beauteous manifestations of the master's teachings. This brief epitome anticipates the story of years. In the course of a long life it was the good fortune of Overbeck to witness the growth into a large tree of the grain of mustard-seed he had cast into the earth.

The Brethren found congenial habitation in the old Franciscan convent of Sant' Isidoro on the Pincian Hill. The picturesque monks having been turned out by Napoleon, the German colony became tenants at a yearly rental, and held in quietude the dormitories, also larger rooms which served as studios, until the fall of the First Empire, when the monastery once more reverted to the Mendicant Friars, by whom it is still occupied. A few years since, the Superior of the Order politely showed the present writer over the ecclesiastical establishment, now, as formerly, devoted to charitable works. Time has brought little change in the cells, the refectory, or in the large hall used for religious teaching. Other rooms, great and small, are ranged round a cloister enclosing a garden still fragrant with orange-blossoms as in the days of Overbeck and Cornelius. Here, amid sacred associations and venerable monuments, did these devoted students build up the new art, and when the day's work was ended, they mounted at eventide the lofty Belvedere, commanding a panorama of which, even in Rome, are few equals. From neighbouring campanili, vesper bells sound a chorus in the bright Italian sky, and beneath the eye stretches, as a prairie of the old world, the wide Campagna, spanned by broken viaducts and bounded by the blue Alban hills. Through the panorama winds the golden Tiber, guarded by the Castle of St. Angelo and St. Peter's, and around and below lie Monte Mario, the pine-clad Pincian, the Villa Medici, and the ilex groves of the Ludovisi. The scene was inspiring, yet not without shadow of melancholy; the Capitol had fallen into the hands of the stranger, but the spirit of Dante fired the dauntless young men; they turned from the present to the past, "imagination restored the empire that had been lost," and though "calamity afflicted the country, they believed that God had not forsaken the people."

Overbeck is known to have been deeply penetrated by the beauties of the Italian sky and landscape. After sufferance of the rigours of northern winters, mind and body expanded under the sun of the genial south. In spring-time came days serene as his own spirit, giving to nature the re-birth he sought for art; the clear horizon carried thought to a world beyond; and in the deep blue above floated such clouds as had served the old pre-Raphaelites with the thrones and footstools of saints and angels. Overbeck did not, as the masters of the decadence, shroud his compositions in backgrounds of impenetrable darkness, but flooded the canvas with the light of the Italian heavens, and like the early painters, placed holy people in the midst of such beauties of nature as tranquillise and elevate the mind. And his sympathetic eye was not only open to scenes which served as distances, he watched in the gardens of the Roman villas the springing flowers, and made careful studies of mossy, jewelled foregrounds which served as carpeting for the feet of his Madonnas. Having turned his back on the Fatherland, his pictures bear no memories of black forests or frowning Harzburg mountains, and he became so thoroughly Italianised that he seated Holy Families on the borders of the Thrasymene Lake, and placed saints within sight of Mount Soracte! Like all true artists, he painted what he saw; as his predecessors, he gathered in daily walks the accessories he needed. Fra Angelico had painted at Fiesole, Francia at Bologna, Perugino at Perugia, Pinturicchio at Spello and Siena, and each in turn, like Overbeck, made the surrounding scenery serve as accompaniments to figure compositions. Nature was to all these painters a great teacher; her presences were healing powers, and they left out all the storms and discords, and like our poet Wordsworth, brought her forms and aspects into harmony with tranquil living. Yet the Brethren from their monastic abode in Sant' Isidoro looked upon the outer world with sympathies as diverse as their individual characters. When Cornelius took his walks abroad, he crossed the Tiber to visit the *Last Judgment* of Michelangelo. Overbeck's steps lay in an opposite direction; he passed by the church of Sta. Maria Maggiore, looked in for the sake of the old mosaics, and then wended his solitary way to Sta. Croce in Gerusalemme, to pay his devotions before the frescoes commemorative of the discovery by St. Helena of the true Cross. Here, in lovely surroundings, nature blended in unison with art, he looked on the blue hills and the calm sky, and thanked God Italy was his home.

The mode of living adopted within the cells and refectory of Sant' Isidoro naturally savoured of the monastic: it combined appropriately society with solitude. The habit of the Brethren was to take meals together at a common table, and to work separately each in his private painting-room. The refectory served as a common hall for study and for drawing from the model. The rule obtained in the establishment that the provisioning and housekeeping should be taken in rotation by each, one week at a time, and it is said that Overbeck had so far a sense of creature comforts that he complained that one of the Brothers was accustomed to put too much water into the broth! On Sundays the work relaxed or ceased wholly, and the wholesome practice prevailed of bringing together the products of the week for criticism with the end to mutual improvement: many grave observations and lively pleasantries passed from one to the other, Overbeck usually in his modest way acting the part of mentor. "No one," writes Schadow, "who saw or heard him speak, could question his purity of motive, his deep insight and abounding knowledge: he is a treasury of art and poetry and a saintly man." Overbeck had stoutly defended the adopted course of study which others condemned. "What," he asked,

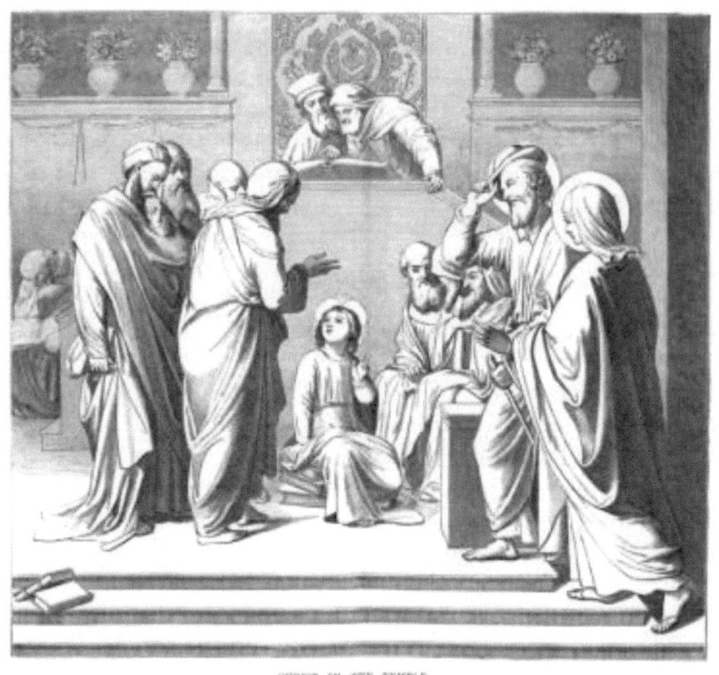

"has been our crime? It is in great measure that we have striven after a severe outline, in opposition to the loose, cloudy, washed-out manner of the day. Is not this an endeavour after truth?" But such studies, while filling portfolios, brought no grist to the mill. And the historian Niebuhr, an anxious friend, confesses that these devoted men "were hard put to it for their daily bread," yet never has a confraternity of artists more nearly approached an ideal. No vow was actually taken, the bond was simply voluntary; thus Overbeck expressly states, "with the greatest concord among us as to the fundamental principles of art, each goes on his own way."

The attitude assumed almost of necessity provoked opposition, even ridicule. The assumption was made of superiority, the tone grew even assailant; Correggio, Guido, Guercino, and Domenichino, with all post-Raphaelites, were denounced, and not only was it declared, "We are right," but it was added, "You are wrong." The Brethren personally laid themselves open to attack; they were not free from the affectations of youth, they made themselves conspicuous by long hair and strange costume, and through their exclusiveness and sanctity won as their nickname the epithet of "Nazarites." Other designations were less characteristic; simply descriptive are such terms as "pre-Raphaelites," "the new-old School," "the German-Roman artists," "the Church-Romantic painters," "the German patriotic and religious painters." But all trivial imputations weigh lightly when set in the balance against solid work and holy living. The earnest devotees in the long run silenced evil tongues and won respect and a good name. Niebuhr, ambassador and historian, by no means a blind apologist, describing the art society of the day, writes: "The painters in Rome are divided by a broad line of demarcation into two parties—the one consisting of our friends and their adherents, the other of the united phalanx of those who are of the world, a set who intrigue and lie and backbite; they intend there shall not be light, come what will. The former are exemplary in their lives; the latter display the old licentiousness which characterised the German artists in Rome thirty years ago. Happily, at the present moment, the more talented of the newcomers are ranged on the side of our friends. It is a hopeful sign that some foreigners, and even Italians, are beginning to pay attention to their works." Overbeck and his more immediate associates were indeed, in the best sense of the term, "purists" and "pietists," and held vitally to the maxim that they who would know of a doctrine must live out the doctrine. On no other conditions was it possible to accomplish their mission—the regeneration of art. The schools around them had fallen in great measure through lack of sincerity and truth; they in contrast believed as our English Bishop Butler taught, that conscience is the ruling faculty in the human mind.

The style of art dominant in Rome during Overbeck's early residence did not materially differ from that which he had left behind him in Vienna. The Director, in fact, of the Viennese Academy had in youth won the prize of Rome, and there became the representative of the prevailing decadence. Among the Italians, Battoni, following in the footsteps of Carlo Maratti, was not without the grace and the beauty of Correggio and Guido. Descending a generation later, Overbeck found among his contemporaries Pietro Benvenuto, one of the most distinguished adherents of the school of David: whose masterpiece in Arezzo Cathedral has justly been designated "one of the finest productions of modern art." These were not men to be wholly despised. Furthermore it is to be remembered, as before indicated, that the Germans, in a generation only just passed away, had here in Rome formed a learned school based on the antique; Lessing, in his treatise, the 'Laocoon,' and Winckelmann, by his criticisms on the marbles of the Vatican, had induced a new Classic Renaissance. The painter Raphael Mengs, thus guided, appropriately executed in the Villa Albani the famous fresco of *Apollo and the Nine Muses on Mount Parnassus*. Again, here are men and manifestations not to be disdained. But for such art Overbeck, as we have seen, cherished inveterate antipathy: whether he was absolutely right, impartial critics, founding a judgment on a wide historic basis, will hesitate to determine. The correct verdict probably is that each school is good of its kind, that the one possesses merits distinctive of the other, and that it is well for the world that every mode of thought should in turn obtain the fullest and highest manifestation. But Overbeck's vision was too intently focussed on one point to perceive that his sphere was but a segment, a part, though by no means an unimportant part, of the greater whole. The classic movement, against which he set his face steadily, was not to be easily annihilated; it survived in Rome in such illustrious representatives as Canova, Thorwaldsen and Gibson. But Overbeck grew more and more the recluse; he shortly became a proselyte to the Romish Church, shut himself out from other associations, and thus after a time devoted his pencil exclusively to Christian Art.

The early pictures and drawings executed in Rome carry out the painter's resolve. To this first period belong: *The Adoration of the Kings* (1811), *Jesus in the House of Martha and Mary* (1812), *The Preaching of St. John, The Raising of Lazarus, The Entombment, Christ Blessing Little Children, The Holy Family, Ave Maria, Blessed art thou among Women*, also a portrait of Vittoria Caldoni.[2] The first commission received by the struggling painter came from Queen Caroline of Bavaria for *The Adoration of the Kings*, in oils. The Queen had written to Rome saying that she wished for a picture by the young artist; that as to the price, a hard bargain need not be driven, for when one gains a beautiful work, the cost cannot be regretted. Overbeck, on receiving the good news, writes, December

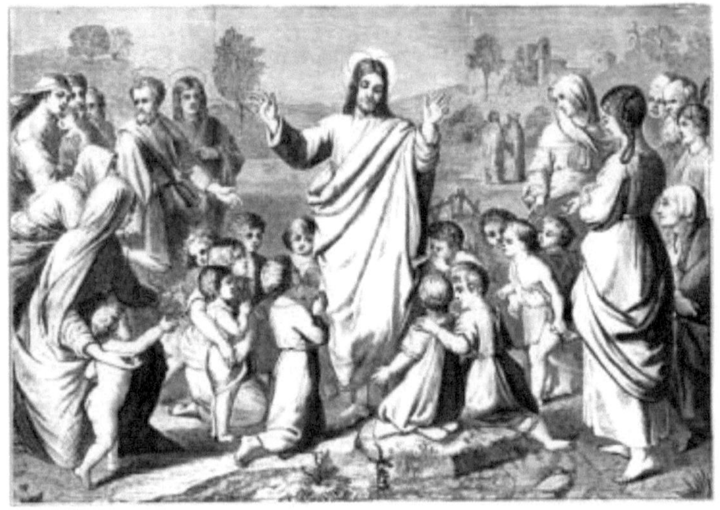

CHRIST BLESSING LITTLE CHILDREN.

16, 1811, "I was so overpowered with joy that I could not bring out a syllable. The affair moves me all the more because I had not dreamt of it. What can be the cause of my good fortune? Happy day! I shall think of it as long as I live: to the Lord be the praise." Four days later he writes to Lübeck: — "What joy! I can now relieve my parents from further burden. This is the moment so long wished for. Henceforth and for ever I am a man and an independent artist in the workshop, free as a king over the boundless domain of fantasy to create a beautiful world."

The maxim that correct drawing lies at the foundation of all true art was maintained by the Brotherhood through both precept and example. Overbeck first mastered form, he trained his hand to out-line; next he learnt the principles of composition, that is the power of combining separate parts into a connected whole; lastly, he added colour, but rather as an accessory than an essential. Hence his water-colours and even his oil-pictures are often little more than tinted drawings. In the first Roman period, that is up to about the year 1820, when the age of thirty had been reached, we find the artist in full possession of the faculty of expressing his ideas at the point of his pencil. Of this happy facility many examples have come before me: one especially, at Stift Neuburg, *The Raising of Jairus's Daughter* (1814); another, almost a replica of the last, delicately washed with colour, in the private collection of Herr Malss, of the Städel Institute, Frankfort. I note with admiration the precision and subtlety of the form, especially in the hands and feet. The work, though small in scale (1 ft. 3 in. by 1 ft.), is large in manner, the treatment being that of the Great Masters as distinguished from the Small Masters. Overbeck, who was on intimate terms with the family of Director Malss, said that he wished they should have a work as perfect as he could make it: verily he realised his endeavour. Belonging to the same period, I find in another private collection in Frankfort a portrait in delicate pencilling of a young girl of about eighteen; the hair is in close curls all round the head, the necklace is marked with utmost detail. Perhaps I have not laid sufficient stress on the truth and rectitude of Overbeck's work, as seen, for instance, in the *Head of an Old Monk* among the drawings of the National Gallery, Berlin. This is so close to nature that a deformity in one ear has been conscientiously registered. The handling here is masterly, the touch firm and strong; the play of lines in the hatchings proves a free hand and a facile turn of the wrist. Also may be mentioned, for incidents taken from the life, a remarkable composition at Stift Neuburg, *The Feeding of the Hungry*. Close to nature are these transcripts of the poor, the needy, and aged, one advancing on crutches to receive bounty; and over all presides the spirit of beauty and charity. Also in the same collection is a triptych, wherein angels and cherubs appear: this is among the earliest examples of the intervention of the supernatural. Overbeck was not the man to rush in where angels fear to tread. Likewise among Biblical subjects, I find in the National Gallery, Berlin, *The Creation of Adam and Eve*, and *The Expulsion from Paradise*. Here the delineation of the undraped figure proves absolute knowledge, and shows, as before said, that the usual course of drawing from the nude had been gone through. The point indeed need not be discussed further, as Schadow expressly states that Overbeck's drawings from the nude as well as from the draped figure were, for subtlety and truth to nature, the admiration of every one. The *Creation* and *Expulsion* are of exceptional value, because the artist for once borrows from Michelangelo: also it will be seen that Overbeck gave himself from the outset to the illustration of the Biblical narrative, and thus fondly trod in the footsteps of Giotto and Fra Angelico.

An Exhibition of the works of the German painters in Rome was held in 1819, in a room of the Palazzo Caffarelli, which, as the official residence of Niebuhr and Bunsen, had often been a spot of kindly meeting and hospitality. The collection Frederick Schlegel pronounced unsurpassed in richness, variety, and intrinsic value. Public interest was awakened, and attention centred round the contributions of Overbeck, Schadow, Veit and Cornelius. Overbeck sent a *Madonna* and a *Flight into Egypt*; and Schlegel specially names the cartoon of *Jerusalem Delivered*, for the frescoes then in progress at the Villa Massimo, as proof of the artist's power of expression and faculty of invention. He adds: "The struggle of the German artists in Rome daily excites more and more observation, and their progress is watched with cordial sympathy by men of all nations."

A very serious topic must now be considered. Overbeck in 1813 relinquished the Protestant faith of his forefathers and joined the Roman Catholic Church. Obviously in these pages polemics are out of place, and the step which the conscientious painter thought fit to take has to be here noted so far only as it serves as an index to character and as an interpretation of art. Rightly to judge the case, it were well correctly to estimate Overbeck as a man: his strength lay within his art, outside which he had infirmities; his bodily health was feeble, his mind to the extreme refined and to the last degree sensitive; he shrank from the conflict of life; common people he could not associate with; for the ordinary world he was wholly unfit, and sought refuge in some ideal not yet reached. Niebuhr truly reads the character when he writes: "Overbeck is an enthusiast and quite illiberal; he is a very amiable man and endowed with a magnificent imagination, but incapable by nature of standing alone, and by no means so clear-headed as he is poetical. He bends easily and naturally under the yoke of the Catholic faith."

Overbeck doubtless felt all the more need of safe anchorage from the sea of troubles on which many minds were cast through the controversy and scepticism which agitated Protestant Europe. In Lübeck, as we have seen, the phases of faith were philosophic and æsthetic, and the divinities of Olympus and Parnassus shared equal favour with the saints of the Church. The young painter was cast in a severer mould, and needed that the infinite and eternal should be circumscribed by definite form. It is reported of a certain German philosopher that, when addressing his class, he ended with the words: — "In the next lecture we shall proceed to construct God!" Overbeck preferred to such speculation the authority of the Church. The painter Joseph Führich puts the case strongly:[3] he declares that his friend had to take the choice between Pantheism and Catholicism. Overbeck felt that art was a religious question, and he determined that all his work should be a protest against the indifferentism and latitudinarianism which account all religions equal. He conceded that secular writings and mundane arts were not without their value and charm; in the arts may be permitted divers manifestations, such as landscape, animal, and flower painting. The Church is tolerant of all that is good, but on the highest pinnacle stands the Christian painter. Over these matters he had pondered long, and was accustomed to say to himself, "Let not my Christ be ever robbed of my love; the true home of art is within the soul before the altar of the Church; the tabernacle of art has its foundations in the worship of God."

Early Christian Art naturally drew Overbeck towards the Roman Catholic Church. Frederick Schlegel, Rio, Pugin severally fell under the same spell. The old mosaics, frescoes, and easel pictures which came down through unbroken ecclesiastical descent, were for the Christian artist of the nineteenth century means of grace, and served as revelations of the Divine. Fra Angelico was taken as a pattern; through living and loving, watching and praying, believing and working, the High Priesthood of Art was to be established. And the actual experiences of modern Rome brought no disillusion; the frivolity and the hollowness which so often disgust newcomers were either not seen or were turned aside from. The painter was too pure and childlike to realise the evil, he turned only to the good: for him the world shone as a land of light; from art he would exorcise the passions; the true art-life blended heaven with earth, the ideal could be attained only through the Church: her teachings were the education of humanity.

The decisive step ultimately taken is recorded as follows: "Overbeck at Whitsuntide in the year 1813 joined the Catholic Faith, and with joy entered into the family of the world's Church. His spiritual guide and confessor was Professor, afterwards Cardinal, Ostini; and the poet Zacharias Werner, of Königsberg, as a fellow-countryman from the shores of the northern sea, acted as godfather at the ceremony. The poet, in writing at the time to the Prince Primate of Dalberg, said that he recognised in the young painter 'a true seraphic character of the Fatherland.'"[4]

A veritable mental epidemic seized on the German artists, and when one after another of Overbeck's friends followed his example, Niebuhr took alarm, and bethought himself of what measures could be taken. It appears that a pamphlet had been published intended expressly for the conversion of the young Germans, and Niebuhr, feeling the emergency of the situation, requested a friend to bring or send Luther's works with other writings against Popery. He adds: "It cannot be expressed how disgusting these proceedings become the more you see of them. At this moment the proselytes have Schadow, one of the ablest of the young artists, on their bait." At a later date he writes: "I like Overbeck and the two Schadows much, and they are estimable both as artists and as men; but the Catholicism of Overbeck and one of the Schadows excludes entirely many topics of conversation." Overbeck is elsewhere described as of "very prepossessing physiognomy, taciturn and melancholy," with a "proselyting spirit." Bunsen, who no less than Niebuhr deplored these conversions, writes in 1817 that Overbeck had been for a fortnight in August a welcome guest at Frascati, that he had finished a water-colour drawing—a very lovely Madonna with the infant Jesus—"of which he permitted a copy to be taken, still extant, and valued as a record of the time and of the short-lived intimacy with the gentle and heavenly-minded artist, who soon after this period withdrew from all companions of a different religious persuasion from that which he had adopted." Among the chief converts are numbered the brothers Schadow, Veit, Platner, and the critic Frederick Schlegel. Cornelius is not included, because he was born into Catholicism. He is described as of "an open and powerful intellect, free from all limitations," "with habits and convictions rooted as the facts of his existence." He thus looked on coolly while the new converts were at fever-heat. Yet it is pleasant to know that these controversies were, in the main, preserved from personal bitterness, and that whatever might be the difference in creeds, the broad union of religion and humanity was never torn asunder. Thus in 1817 Niebuhr, a Protestant and possibly something more, was able to write: "I associate chiefly, indeed almost exclusively, with the artists who belong to the religious party, because those who are decidedly pious, or who strive after piety, are by far the noblest and best men, and also the most intellectual, and this gives me an opportunity of hearing a good deal on faith and its true nature." And the faith of these men we know to have brought forth good works; as were their belief and their practice, such were their pictures, and it is scarcely here the place to discuss whether larger views might have given to their art wider extension.

By a curious coincidence, about the time when these conversions to Roman Catholicism were going on in Rome the third jubilee of the Reformation was celebrated at Lübeck. The pietist father of the painter made himself champion of the cause, and delivered a speech at a meeting of the Bible Society, wherein he proclaimed Luther the great witness of truth. "Luther," he declared, "spoke, wrote, thundered, and the power of darkness was overturned; thus conscience became free, doctrines were purified, and the precious Bible, as a heavenly treasure, was given back to the people."[5] It has been assigned as a reason why Overbeck never returned home, that he could not bear to see the city of Lübeck with her old walls thrown down; but a less fanciful cause was that other walls than those of brick and mortar had been set up, dividing kindred and friends.

Let us now turn from polemics to the pleasing descriptions given by Niebuhr and Bunsen of the daily lives of the German Brotherhood. It is not always that archæologists and literary men are the soundest counsellors of artists; they place overmuch stress on the inward conception and motive; they lay down, like Coleridge, the axiom that "a picture is an intermediate something between a thought and a thing," and in exalting the "thought" they subordinate the "thing." This was the last teaching that Overbeck needed. He and his fellows were already only too prone to ignore technique, to neglect colour, chiaroscuro, texture. They deemed it all-sufficient to perfect form as the language of thought; consequently while their works instruct and elevate, they fail to please or to gain wide popularity.

Nevertheless, taken for all in all, Overbeck and Cornelius must be accounted most fortunate in their intellectual companionship. The habit was, when gathered socially together at the Embassy in the Palazzo Caffarelli, to read books, talk of pictures, and to consort together generally for the furtherance of the great art revival in which Niebuhr and Bunsen believed fervently. The attachment became mutual, the intercourse was prized on both sides. Niebuhr writes of Cornelius and his wife: "They are, strictly speaking, intimate family friends;" and again he says: "The society of Cornelius and Overbeck gives an inspiring variety to the day's occupations, and one or other of these intellectual companions seldom fails to join our evening walks." In another letter we read: "Cornelius of Düsseldorf, Platner from Leipzig, Koch from the Tyrol, Overbeck from Lübeck, Mosler from Coblentz, and William Schadow from Berlin, were assembled at Bunsen's in the apartments of the painter Brandis: in different ways and degrees we are attached to them all, and we think them men of talent. Their society is the only pleasure we derive from human beings in Rome." The young artists are found to be wholly without worldly wisdom, a charge to which at least Overbeck might readily plead guilty. Niebuhr further declares: "I confidently believe we are on the eve of a new era of Art in Germany, similar to the sudden bloom of our literature in the eighteenth century." He discerned in the movement an unaccustomed spiritual phenomenon—one of those manifestations of the national mind from time to time found in the history of humanity. He felt once more an outburst of the intellectual life of Germany, a rising again of the force of genius which had impelled Lessing, Kant, and Goethe, which had given birth to profound philosophy and science, and had animated a whole people with patriotism and a spirit of self-sacrifice to do battle amid national songs and hymns, even to the death, in the cause of the King and the Fatherland. Bunsen testifies how Niebuhr showed his affection and care for the Prussian and German disciples of art; he considered it an agreeable part of his duty and vocation to render them assistance, to encourage them in their studies, to give them the time of which he was so sparing to men of mere show and fashion, also to render them pecuniary assistance when necessary. To Niebuhr belongs the honour of having been the first to recognise the new school at the moment when it was "despised, derided, and vituperated." He befriended the men who had to fight their way against shallowness and wickedness, against the low and false taste of connoisseurs and patrons, till the day came when the martyrs of an exalted aspiration gained the attention and admiration of the world.

Nor in numbering friends must be forgotten Frederick Schlegel, the avowed champion of the new school. The critic was not without connecting links and antecedents; he had made himself son-in-law of the Jewish philosopher Moses Mendelssohn, and stepfather of the painter Philip Veit; and he further qualified himself for his critical duties by joining the Roman Catholic Church. Overbeck and this rhapsodist on Christian Art were naturally close allies; each was of use to the other, and gave and received in turns. The artist strove, it is said, to embody in pictorial form his friend's teachings; the two, in fact, moved in parallel lines. Schlegel urged that the new style must be emulative and aspiring, ever possessed of lofty ideas. Believe not, he writes, that the glory of art has passed away. The hope is not vain that there comes a rekindling of former fires; art uprising from the dark night breaks as the morning's dawn; "a new life can spring only from the depths of a new love." Let us hold that Art like Nature renews her youth. The soul alone can comprehend the truly beautiful; the eye gazes but on the material veil—the union of the inner soul with the outward form constitutes the noblest art. Nowhere are to be found more eloquent utterances on "the Bond between Art and the Church," but in all is overlooked the simple fact that "the Celestial light" cannot be made appreciable to mortal eye otherwise than through the medium of matter, and according to the laws of vision. And to such oversight is greatly to be ascribed the infirmities of Overbeck and his school. It is forgotten that the most holy of motives cannot save a picture which is not good as a picture.

Schlegel discusses the question, What is needed by the Christian painter? The following phrenzy, though wordy, is worth reading:—

"The answer is that the beautiful truths of the Christian faith should not be received into the mind as merely lifeless forms, in passive acquiescence to the teaching of others: they must be embraced with an earnest conviction of their truth and reality, and bound up with each individual feeling of the painter's soul. Still even the influence of devotion is not alone sufficient; for however entirely religion may be felt to compensate for all that is wanting to our earthly happiness, much more is required to form a painter. I know not how better to designate that other element, without which mere technical skill, and even correct ideas, will be unavailing, than by calling it the inborn light of inspiration. It is something quite distinct from fertility of invention, or magic of colouring, rare and valuable as is the latter quality in painting. It is no less distinct from skill in the technicalities of design and from the natural feeling for beauty inherent in some susceptible minds. The poet and the musician should also be inspired, but their inspiration is more the offspring of human emotion; the painter's inspiration must be an emanation of celestial light: his very soul must, so to speak, become itself illumined, a glowing centre of holy radiance, in whose bright beams every material object should be reflected; and even his inmost conceptions and daily thoughts must be interpenetrated by its brightness and remodelled by its power. This indwelling light of the soul should be recognised in every creation of his pencil, expressive as a spoken word; and in this lies the peculiar vitality of Christian beauty, and the cause of the remarkable difference between Classic and Christian art." "Physical beauty is employed by the Christian painter but as a material veil, from beneath which the hidden divinity of the soul shines forth, illuminating all mortal life with the higher spirituality of love."

A kindly and timely commission came to the masters of the German Brotherhood — Overbeck, Cornelius, Veit, and Schadow — from the Prussian Consul, Bartholdi. Personal relations, with the desire of giving the untried painters an opportunity of proving what good was in them, prompted the charge to decorate with frescoes a room in the Casa Bartholdi, situated on the brow of the Pincian Hill.[6] The Prussian Consul was in a roundabout way connected with Philip Veit and Frederick Schlegel, whose mutual relationship has been already recounted; his wife was sister of the philosopher Moses Mendelssohn, and aunt of the illustrious musician, and sundry intermarriages had made, as it were, a compact in literature and art between the families of Bartholdi, Mendelssohn, Veit, and Schlegel.[7] The chosen sphere of operations was comparatively narrow; the small room in an upper story, now of historic interest, is not more than twenty-four feet square. The situation is inviting; the beauties of nature are usually found proximate with the beauties of art, and here the windows command a panorama sweeping from the Pincian to the Tiber, and embracing St. Peter's, the Vatican, St. Angelo, and the Capitol. The topic chosen for these wall pictures was the *Story of Joseph and his Brethren*—a theme conveniently accommodating to any existing diversities in creeds or styles. The technical process adopted was fresco, a monumental art, the revival of which formed part of the mission of the German fraternity. The arduous undertaking was commenced and carried out in strict accordance with historic precedents. Preliminary studies were made, and well-matured cartoons on the scale of the ultimate pictures were perfected. To the lot of Overbeck fell *Joseph sold by his Brethren*,[8] and *The Seven Years of Famine*.

It has been my pleasure to visit and revisit these wall-paintings over a period of a quarter of a century, and growing experience does but enhance my admiration. They fulfil the first requirements of wall decoration: the story is told lucidly and concisely; the style is simple, noble; accidents are held subordinate to essentials; the compositions are distributed symmetrically; the colour, though a little crude, is brought into somewhat agreeable unity; the light and shade are not focussed at one point, but carried evenly over the whole surface; and the treatment inclines sufficiently to the flat to keep the compositions down on the wall. The finished pictures of the four masters vary in dimensions. The lengths range from eight to seventeen feet, the height is mostly about eight feet; the figures do not exceed five feet. The lines bounding the figures and draperies are firm and incisive. Accordant with the practice of the old fresco-painters, each day's work is marked and discernible by the joinings in the plaster, and the junctions between the dry plaster of one day and the wet plaster of the next are appropriately fixed at the points where the subject breaks off readily and can be resumed most easily. The technique is thoroughly mastered, and, barring some surface cracks, the paintings are in as perfect condition as when they came from the artists' hands. The chief defect is a somewhat crude opacity of pigments, a characteristic belonging to the debased period of wall-painting rather than to the *"fresco buono et puro"* of Giotto, Luini, and Pinturicchio.

Another point to be remarked is that the frescoes in the Casa Bartholdi show that the four painters—Overbeck, Cornelius, Veit, and Schadow—worked here at the outset of their career in remarkable unison. In the course of years they diverged widely, but as yet the school collectively dominates over the artist individually. The Brethren had formed themselves equally on the same originals, and had scarcely found time to take their several departures from nature. Indeed, the actual presence of nature comes almost as a surprise in these compositions. Overbeck's figures are manifestly more or less studied from the life, only, according to his habitual practice, he has taken pains to eliminate from his models any individual accidents which marred the generic form, softening down angularity and ruggedness into pervading grace and beauty. Here and there are traces of affectation, together with a feebleness incident to the painter's weak physique which stands in utmost contrast with the force of Cornelius. Overbeck mostly shunned action and dramatic intensity, and here the figures in their movements depart but slightly from the equilibrium of repose. As a religious artist, the New Testament was more within his sphere than the Old. Thus the outrage committed against Joseph by his brethren is toned down into a calm, orderly transaction; placidity reigns throughout; all is brought into keeping with the painter's spirit of gentleness.

The Casa Bartholdi frescoes,[9] when finished, produced a most favourable impression in Rome; the cause of the Germans was greatly strengthened, and the opposite party felt the defeat. The Italians, too, were taken by surprise to find themselves beaten by foreigners on their own ground. A natural consequence of the success was further commissions, and the fortune no less than the fame of the revivalists was made. Singularly enough the modern Romans came forward as the next patrons. Niebuhr, writing from Rome in 1817, says: "It is a significant fact that some foreigners, even Italians, are beginning to pay attention to the works of our friends." It is well known that the Romans had been addicted for centuries to mural painting in palaces, villas and garden-houses: Raphael was employed to decorate the Farnesina; Guido and Annibale Carracci painted the ceilings of the Farnese and of the Rospigliosi Palaces. Emulating these illustrious examples, Prince Massimo commissioned Overbeck, Cornelius, Veit, and Schnorr to cover the walls and ceilings of his Garden Pavilion near St. John Lateran with frescoes illustrative of Tasso, Dante, and Ariosto. Not only the themes, but the local surroundings were inspiring. The Villa Massimo is a site only possible in Rome. When the artists in the morning came to work, before their view opened a panorama embracing the Claudian Aqueduct, St. John Lateran, the Church of Sta. Croce in Gerusalemme, the old Walls of Rome, with cypresses and stone pines around, and the Alban Hills beyond. The Pavilion assigned to the painters stands in the Villa garden, with the accustomed growth and fragrance of orange-trees, magnolias, azaleas, roses, and violets. Overbeck entered on the work with poetic ardour.

The Massimo Pavilion is little more than three rooms standing on the ground; the first, indeed, is an Entrance Hall, and therein Schnorr painted copiously from Ariosto. On the left a door leads to the room assigned to Cornelius for the illustration of Dante: the ceiling fell to the lot of Veit. On the right another door opens to a corresponding room of like dimensions, set apart to Overbeck and Tasso's *Jerusalem Delivered*.[10] This small interior is not more than fifteen feet square, and the wall-spaces are much broken up by doors and windows, so that only one of the four sides remained disencumbered. The compositions are eleven in number, and are unequal alike in size and merit. The largest and most noteworthy is fifteen feet long by ten feet high, representing the *Meeting of Godfrey de Bouillon and Peter the Hermit*. The narrative is lucidly told, the picture well put together, and the successive planes of distance are duly marked. Altogether the fundamental principles of wall-decoration are clearly understood in this the most complex composition yet attempted by the painter. Another thoroughly studied design is *Sophronio and Olindo on the Funeral Pyre delivered by Clorinda*.[11] The action has more than usual force and movement, and the undraped figures are drawn with severe exactitude. Presiding over the whole series, in the middle of the ceiling, is an allegorical figure of *Jerusalem Delivered*.[12] An angel on either side unlooses the fetters of an innocent placid maiden crowned with thorns. These frescoes, notwithstanding their situation in a cold, damp garden-house, remained, when I saw them last, in January, 1878, in sound condition: thus once more we find Overbeck, equally with Cornelius, to have been solidly grounded in the method of wall-painting.

I must confess that I have always been disappointed with this Tasso Room.[13] One reason is that the carrying out of the original designs was delegated to an inferior brush. Overbeck was not in strong health; he worked slowly, and when other commissions came in, some more to his liking, such as that for the church picture at Assisi, he felt overburdened, and wished to be released from a task that had grown wearisome. The work, began about 1817, had dragged on for ten years, till at last Overbeck made a deliberate call on good and friendly Joseph Führich, and requested that he would complete the unfinished frescoes. The proposal, naturally felt as an honour, was gratefully acceded to. After this distance of time it becomes difficult to determine how far this worthy substitute must be held responsible for much that is to be regretted on these walls. For some of the compositions the master had made nothing more than sketches or indications, and at least three must be laid to the charge of the scholar. Führich was for Overbeck what Giulio Romano had been for Raphael, and the Tasso Room suffered the same degradation as the latest stanza in the Vatican.

The Tasso Room may be taken as a measure of Overbeck's capacity. This "cyclus," or series, shows the painter's power of sustained thought and faculty of invention. Much, doubtless, is compilation, yet something remains of originality. The best passages are those not borrowed from old pictures, but taken from life, which makes the regret all the greater that here and in the sequel nature was not trusted more implicitly. On the whole, these compositions leave the impression that Overbeck had not mental force or physical stamina sufficient for the task. It is true that the presence of a lyrical spirit is felt; but scenes of Romance need more fire and passion; the deeds of Chivalry were not enacted in a cloister. Perhaps self-knowledge wisely counselled Overbeck to quit the regions of creative imagination. With greater peace of mind he trod in the future, the safer paths of Christian Art, wherein precedent and authority served as his guide and support.

FOOTNOTES:

[1] See among other authorities: 'Die Deutsche Kunst in unserem Jahrhundert, von Dr. Hagen,' vol. ix. Berlin, 1857.

[2] The above compositions suggest the following observations. Overbeck was in the habit of making over many years replicas with variations and improvements of favourite themes, and the dates of the successive stages are not always easily determined. Of the *Preaching of St. John*, the Düsseldorf Academy possesses an example dated 1831. Also in the same collection is a mature and almost fault-less drawing, fit companion for Raphael, of *The Raising of Lazarus*; the figure of Christ is 9 inches high. Overbeck made several render-ings of the universally-beloved composition, *Christ Blessing Little Children*: the most deliberate is that given in these pages. The replica in the Meyer Collection, Hamburg, is of the last decade of the artist's life, and betrays infirmity of hand. *The Entombment*, classed above among works of the first Roman period, is probably that now in the choice collection at Stift Neuburg, near Heidelberg, dated 1814, and obviously suggested by Raphael's *Entombment* in the Bor-ghese Palace. No drawings have better pedigree than those in this old family mansion: a predecessor of the present possessor was the artist's personal friend. The version of *The Bearing to the Sepulchre* given in these pages is from one of the forty well-known drawings of the Gospels, and dates 1844. At Stift Neuburg I also saw in the autumn of 1880, by the courtesy of the owner, Graf von Bernus, the drawing for the *Holy Family*, chosen as an illustration to this vol-ume; it is of utmost delicacy and beauty—the motive has evidently

been borrowed from Raphael; the measurement is 1 foot 3 inches by 1 foot 8 inches.

[3] See 'Autobiography of Joseph Führich,' published in Vienna and Pesth, 1875.

[4] See 'Historisch-Politische Blätter für das Katholische Deutschland,' vol. lvi., part 8. Munich, 1870.

[5] See 'Erinnerung an Christian Adolph Overbeck;' Lübeck, 1830.

[6] The Casa Bartholdi has for some years been let as lodgings to a superior class of travellers, and is much favoured by the English. The rooms are not always accessible; the servants have been known to name, as the most convenient time for seeing the frescoes, Sunday mornings, when the tenants are attending the English Church. The Painted Chamber is suitably furnished for daily uses; *The History of Joseph*, which covers the walls, is not too serious a theme to mingle with the common avocations of domestic life: fresco-painting, in fact, is not only a national and an ecclesiastic, but likewise a domestic art.

[7] The Royal Academy Exhibition, Berlin, 1880, contained a large coloured design for the decoration of the ceiling of the Villa Mendelssohn-Bartholdy. Thus the joint names over a period of more than half a century stand conspicuous among art-patrons.

[8] Overbeck's cartoon in charcoal on paper of *Joseph sold by his Brethren* is carefully preserved under glass in the Städel Institute, Frankfort, where I examined it in 1880: the width is 11 feet, the height 8 feet, the figures are about 5 feet. The outlines are firmly accentuated; the details sufficient without being elaborate; the figure, as proved specially in the arms, hands, legs, and feet, is perfectly understood; the draperies are cast simply and broadly; the heads of noble type are impressed with thought. Not a false touch appears throughout; the crayon is guided by knowledge; evidently preliminary studies and tentative drawings must have preceded this consummated product. No wonder that this cartoon made a deep impression; nothing had been seen at all like it in Rome for very many years.

[9] Many are the authors who have written on the Casa Bartholdi frescoes, the chief authorities are Hagen, Förster, Reber, and Riegel.

[10] See among authorities before named, 'Geschichte des Wiederauflebens der deutschen Kunst zu Ende des 18. und Anfang des 19. Jahrhunderts, von Hermann Riegel.' Hannover, 1876.

[11] The cartoon for this fresco is in the Leipzig Museum, where I examined it in 1880. It is in chalk on whity-brown paper, in squares and mounted on canvas; length 15 feet by 7 feet. As a mature study of form and composition it is just what a cartoon should be, but the touch is feeble and poor. Like most of Overbeck's designs, it has received the tribute of engraving.

[12] The cartoon was acquired for the National Gallery, Berlin, in 1878, at the price of 37*l*. 10*s*. 0*d*.; measurement 6 feet by 4 feet: it has been engraved.

[13] Persistent difficulties are placed in the way of even students who desire to visit these frescoes; the public are systematically excluded from the Villa Massimo, and on two occasions, when after much trouble I gained orders for admission, the attendant, in accordance with instructions, forbade the taking of notes.

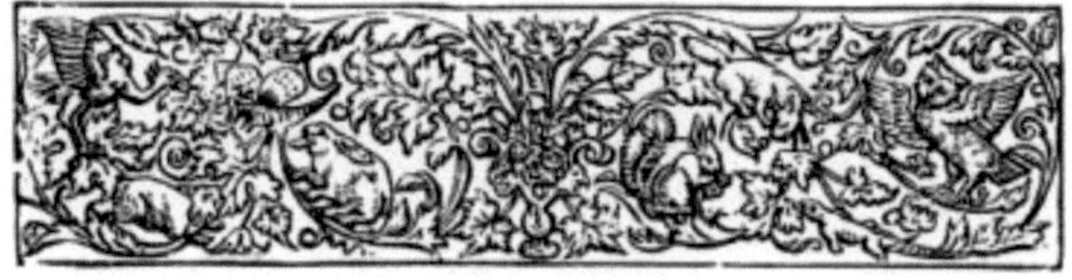

CHAPTER III.

ROME — GERMANY.

THE life of Overbeck apportioned itself into successive periods of five, ten, or more years, corresponding to the important works from time to time in hand. The painter threw his whole mind into whatever he undertook, and so his pictures in their conception, and even in their execution, reflect the thought and the state of consciousness which for the while held supreme sway. The preceding chapters treat of two periods; the one describes the early times in Lübeck and Vienna, the other presents a sketch of the first decade in Rome. The foundations have been laid; the main principles for the guidance of a true life and for the building up of a soul-moving art have been firmly fixed; and now it remains to be seen how far and in what way the lofty aim was reached.

Overbeck, as soon as his prospects in life became somewhat assured, married. Little is recorded of the wife: the earliest mention I have met with is in 1818, when the artists in Rome gave a grand fête in honour of the Crown Prince of Bavaria. Overbeck and Cornelius furnished designs for pictorial decorations and transparencies: the guests wore mediæval costumes, and made themselves

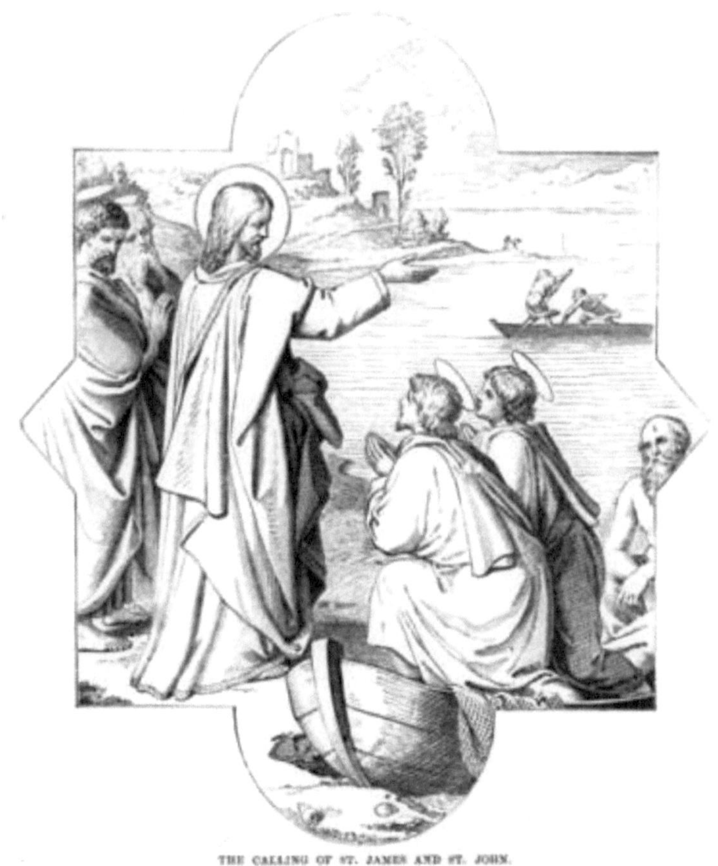

THE CALLING OF ST. JAMES AND ST. JOHN.

otherwise attractive; and we learn on the authority of Madame Bunsen that among the brilliant assembly "the most admired of the evening was Overbeck's future wife, a lady beautiful, engaging, and influential, from Vienna."[1] The marriage, which was not long delayed, proved on the whole happy, though the wife's delicate health gave constant cause for anxiety, and her other demands on an indulgent husband are said to have provoked the displeasure of Cornelius and other friends. Two children were the fruits of the union: a girl, who died young, and a boy, who lived only long enough to give singular promise.

Overbeck, as we have seen, had, in common with his brethren, given his best powers to "monumental painting." For this noble and "architectonic art" he was not without qualifications. He moved in an exalted sphere, his mind ranged among immutable truths, his forms were high in type, his compositions had symmetry and concentration, he knew how to adapt lines and masses to structural spaces. An occasion calculated to call forth his powers came with the commission to paint in fresco *The Vision of St. Francis* for the church of Sta. Maria degli Angeli, near Assisi. Overbeck here, as his custom was, remained obedient to tradition, and yet struck out a new path; he was not content to retrace the footsteps of Giotto or of Cigoli, he preferred to depict the vision of his own mind. He enthrones the Madonna as Queen of Heaven, seated by the side of the risen Saviour, surrounded by the angelic hosts. On the lower earth, also attended by angels, appears St. Francis in adoration, while on the other side kneel reverently two mendicant friars. The picture belongs to the middle period, when the artist had attained the mature age of forty: the style, speaking historically, is that of the grave and severely defined Florentine school as represented by the Brancacci chapel. The fresco has been accounted by some the painter's masterpiece, and it is pronounced by Count Raczynski as one of the few works of modern days worthy of transmission to future ages.[2]

Overbeck, it is easy to believe, while painting on the very spot where St. Francis was in ecstasy, led a life much to his liking. He dwelt within the monastery, and his pure mind, open only to the good, was blind to the dissolute ways of monks who became a scandal to the district. When the fresco was half finished, the master received a visit from his bosom friends Steinle and Führich, and the three strengthened one another as they communed on religion and the arts. Overbeck is known to have had leanings towards a convent life, and at one time, when seriously thinking of taking the vow, he received from the Pope friendly admonition that his true mission lay within his art, and that by renouncing the world his usefulness would be lessened. It can scarcely, however, be doubted that asceticism became so much the habit of his life as to afflict his mental condition, and to impoverish his art. Some critics indeed point to the early picture of *The Seven Years of Famine* as the origin of a certain starved aspect in subsequent compositions. Pharaoh's lean kine have been supposed to symbolise the painter, and the spare fare within the cells of St. Francis served to confirm the persuasion that flesh and blood, in art as in life, must be kept in subjection. Nevertheless, I for one, when on the spot, could not but revere the pictorial outcome; when first I made acquaintance with this plenary revelation of the painter, I had been taking a walking-tour, knapsack on back, through the Umbrian hills and valleys, the birth-land of St. Francis; I had become acquainted with the wall and panel paintings of Giotto, Gentile di Fabriano, Perugino, Giovanni Santi, and the youthful Raphael; and while looking on this heavenly "Vision," I could not but feel that Overbeck ranked among the holy company. Unlike most modern painters, surely he had not to worship in the outer court of the Gentiles.

Overbeck received repeated solicitations to return to Germany: he was asked in 1821 by Cornelius to take the directorship of the Düsseldorf Academy, and four years later he writes in reply to the further persuasions of Wintergerst and Mosler. He urges his incapacity for the duties: he had learnt painting, he says, in a way difficult to impart to others; moreover, sculpture and architecture he did not understand at all, and as for the business matters he was without faculty. Further difficulties were the health of his wife and the welfare of his son: "every information," he continues, "I receive from my native country tells me of spiritual fermentations: the sanctuary, insufficiently protected by the law, suffers under attacks, and a proud worldly spirit raises its head and proclaims its wisdom. Can parents be blind to the risks to which they expose their child, till now reared in the most delightful simplicity of belief? Dearest friends, can you give us the assurance that we shall be able to educate our son in the simple Catholic faith which we have learnt to recognise as the most vital and consoling." Overbeck, it need hardly be added, shrank from the dangers and declined the duties.

But, at length, free from pressing and onerous commissions, he lent a more willing ear to invitations from Germany. Cornelius in 1830 had come to Rome from Munich, the better to complete certain cartoons; with him were a daughter, also his wife, who had under charge Fräulein Emilie Linder, a young lady of Basle, of some means and given to pictorial pursuits. Overbeck, on the completion of his wall-painting at Assisi, rejoined the brilliant art circle of the Roman capital, and from this time dates the memorable friendship between the lady, then a Protestant, and the great Catholic painter. After a winter pleasantly passed among congenial spirits, the whole party in the early summer of 1831 set out from Rome and reached Florence. Emilie Linder returned for a time to Basle, while Overbeck, under the care of Cornelius, by way of the Tyrol reached Munich. On the news of their approach in July, the local artists, young and old, assembled at the gates, outposts had been stationed along the road, and the townfolks gathered by thousands in the streets: from afar the cheering was heard, and then group after group raised the cry, "Overbeck!" "Cornelius!" The entry soon grew into a triumphal march, and, protests notwithstanding, the horses were unyoked, and a company of lusty youths drew the carriage to the dwelling of Cornelius.

Twenty years had elapsed since Overbeck, an unknown youth, had quitted his native land; he now returned with a world-wide reputation. Cornelius, once the sharer of his trials, became the equal recipient of the triumphs; he had just completed the grand series of frescoes for the Glyptothek, and with him were brought the cartoons elaborated in Rome for the wall-paintings in the new Ludwig Kirche. Overbeck, as the guest of his old friend, passed happy weeks in Munich. The two painters conferred closely together in the interests of Christian Art, and aided each other in the arduous works soon to be carried out. The artists of Bavaria signalised the visit of the apostle of Christian Painting by a jubilee; they gave in honour of the illustrious stranger one of those joyous and scenic fêtes for which Munich is famed. The locality chosen was the Starnberger See, a lovely region of hill and lake lying in the Bavarian highlands, bordering on the Ammergau, peopled by peasants with sacred traditions since better known through "The Passion Play." Overbeck writes gratefully of enjoyment and instruction received through kind friends among the beauties of nature and of art.

The Roman recluse in his journey northwards had widely extended his knowledge of nature. On leaving the Apennines he encountered the Alps, and exchanged beauty for grandeur. His figures were often accompanied by landscapes; but mountains exceeding in altitude five or six thousand feet appalled his imagination; masses of such magnitude could not enter the smaller sphere of his consciousness; hence his northern peregrinations brought into his compositions no Alpine presences; indeed, his habitual serenity and simplicity were disturbed by dramatic stir or storm of the elements, and though his sympathies warmed under novel experiences, his art failed to take a new departure.

I have often when in Munich regretted that Overbeck had no share in the Bavarian manifestations of Christian Art. But that he, the head of the religious revival, is left out was simply his own fault. Cornelius, in 1821, when as director reorganising the Academy, wrote to his friend, asking assistance; King Ludwig also urged Overbeck to come. But the timorous artist as usual hesitated; he gave at first assent, conditional however on a delay of three years to complete works in hand; then he pleaded the impossibility of taking any step whatsoever without the sense of religious duty. The King naturally grew weary, and interpreted the equivocal dealing as a denial. Cornelius again in 1833, when the new Basilica of St. Boniface needed decoration, once more proposed that his fellow-labourer in Rome should settle in Munich, but with no avail; the King evidently had little cordiality for the artist, and so employed others on the plea, not wholly tenable, that Overbeck was better in oil than in fresco. Thus the large acreage of wall surfaces dedicated to Christian Art in the churches of Munich and the Cathedral of Spires fell into the hands of Cornelius, Hess, and Schraudolph. It is impossible not to regret that this grand sphere was thus closed to the artist who of all others had most of beauty to reveal. Yet the sensitive painter might have encountered much to disturb his peace of mind. King Ludwig could not assuredly be quite the patron for a spiritual and esoteric artist, and, moreover, there was something too wholesale in the Munich way of going on for a man of limited strength. Overbeck, as I can testify, was about the last person to climb a giddy ladder or to endure a long day's drudgery before an acreage of wall fifty feet above the ground. He wisely did not overstep his bounds; he had not the wing of an eagle, and preferred to keep as a dove, near to the nest.

Nevertheless, Munich is not without witness to the spirit of the mystic and poetic painter. King Ludwig, himself at least a poetaster, hit upon a felicitous comparison, oft since reiterated, when he designated Overbeck the St. John and Cornelius the St. Paul in pictorial art. The two artists, like the two apostles, had a common faith, though a diverse calling, and their several works testify how greatly the one was indebted to the other. Overbeck brought with him to Bavaria a drawing of exceptional power, *Elias in the Chariot of Fire* (1827), a composition which reflects as indubitably the greatness of Cornelius as Raphael's *Isaiah* responds to the grandeur of Michelangelo. But this lofty strain of inspiration proved transient, and Overbeck, as seen in Munich, truly personates the apostle who leant on the Saviour's breast. The New Pinakothek is fortunate in the possession of three pictures.[3] One is the *Portrait of Vittoria Caldoni*, already enumerated among earliest efforts; another is the *Holy Family*, illustrating these pages; the composition recalls Raphael's Florentine manner. The third, *Italy and Germany*, must be accounted exceptional because secular; the motive, however, rises above common life into symbolism. Two maidens in tender embrace are depicted seated in a landscape, the one blonde and homely, personifying Germania; the other dark and ideal, as if Tasso inspired, typical of Italia. The intention has given rise to interesting speculation. The German girl leans forward in earnest entreaty, while her Italian sister remains immobile and impenetrable. And herein some have seen shadowed forth a divided mind between two nationalities. Solicitations had come from Germany, yet, after moments of hesitation, Overbeck held fast to the land of his adoption, and his resolve may not inaptly find expression in "Italia," a figure which seems to say, "Vex not my spirit; leave me to rest in this land of peace and of beauty." But this composition is supposed to speak of yet wider experiences. The painter had given much time to the writing of a romance descriptive or symbolic of human life, wherein he embodied his own personal feelings and aspirations. The two principal characters in this unpublished story are said to be here depicted under the guise of "Italia and Germania." The composition thus becomes somewhat autobiographic.

Munich is identified with a friendship between Overbeck and a lady, which ranks among the most memorable of Platonic attachments. Fräulein Emilie Linder we have already encountered in Rome, where an abiding friendship was rooted, and the devoted lady, on separation, soon found occasion to open a correspondence which was prolonged over a period of thirty years. Overbeck was a persistent letter-writer; he wasted no time on society, and so gained leisure to write epistles and publish essays. And yet it cannot be said that, had he not been an artist, he would have shone as the brightest of authors. On the contrary, as with the majority of painters, he never acquired an adroitness of pen commensurate with his mastery in the use of his pencil; and it is certain that if his pictures had been without adorers, his prose would have remained without readers. The great painter was destitute of literary style; his sentences are cumbrous and confused; his pages grow wearisome by wordy repetition. Doubtless his thoughts are pure and elevated, but, lacking originality, they run into platitudes, and barely escape commonplace. The prolonged correspondence with Emilie Linder[4] contracts the flavour peculiar to polemics. Overbeck had grown into a "fanatic Catholic"; he was ever casting out nets to catch converts; his tactics were enticing; his own example proved persuasive. Moreover, about his mind and method was something effusive, which won on the hearts of emotional women. At all events, these letters brought over to the Roman Catholic Church the lady and others. And so it naturally came to pass that the bonds of union were drawn very close when the revered apostle and the devout disciple reposed within the same sheepfold. These letters have a further significance; they declare what indeed is otherwise well established, that the Catholic faith served as the prime moving power in the life and the art of Overbeck.

The painter brought to Munich ten or more drawings executed in Rome with a view to his travelling expenses, and Emilie Linder lost no time in making an offer for the set, to add to her private collection. The artist, with suitable diffidence, hesitated, yet looked on the proposal as an interposition of Providence, and then begged for the money at once, to help him on his further journey into Germany. Though success had delivered him from poverty, and commissions came in faster than he could paint, yet at no time did he roll in wealth; spite of scrupulous economy, he never much more than paid his way; and a few years later, when, for Emilie Linder, engaged on *The Death of St. Joseph*,[5] he gladly accepted

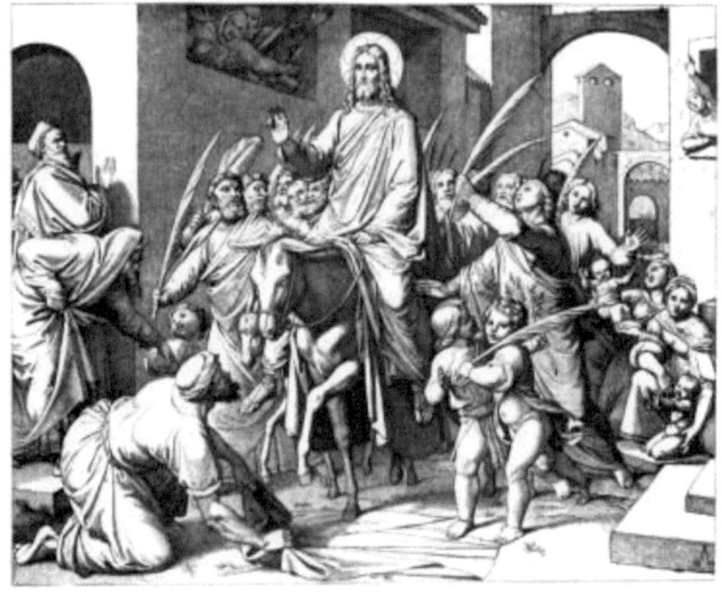

THE ENTRY INTO JERUSALEM.

beforehand the price by instalments. The correspondence shows a tender conscience, with a humility not devoid of independence. The art products were in fact of so high a quality that the painter conferred a greater favour than any he could receive in return.

Overbeck left the hospitable roof of Cornelius in Munich at the end of August, 1831, and reached Heidelberg, there to meet with an enthusiastic reception from friends and admirers; there also, after a separation of five-and-twenty years, he saw once more, and for the last time, his elder brother from Lübeck. Close to Heidelberg, overhanging the banks of the Necker, is Stift Neuburg, formerly a monastic establishment, but then the picturesque residence of a family in warmest bonds of friendship with the art brethren. At this lovely spot, I am told by the present owner, "Overbeck stayed several days, and a seat in the garden is still called after him 'Overbeck's Plätzchen.'" On this rustic bench the painter was wont to sit meditatively amid scenery of surpassing beauty; the quietude of nature and the converse of kindred minds were to his heart's content. Within the old mansion, on the walls and in portfolios, are the choicest examples of the artist's early and middle periods; thus Stift Neuburg in its house and grounds remains sacred to the painter's memory.[6]

From Heidelberg Overbeck travelled to Frankfort—a city soon to become a focus of the wide-spreading revival. Here the apostle of sacred art made the acquaintance of the poet Clemens Brentano, and fell among other friends and adorers. Philip Veit, his fellow-worker in the Casa Bartholdi and the Villa Massimo, had just been appointed Director of the Städel Institute, where he executed one of the noblest of frescoes—*The Introduction of the Arts into Germany through Christianity*. Likewise among warm adherents was Johann Passavant, a painter who in Rome had joined the brethren, a critic who made a name by the 'Life of Raphael.' Overbeck was here esteemed "the greatest living artist," and some expressed "the cherished thought, the earnest desire" that the painter should be secured for Frankfort. But as this proved out of the question, the promise was gladly accepted of the master-work since famous as *The Triumph of Religion in the Arts*. Cologne next received a visit, and the Cathedral choir having advanced towards completion, the assistance of the Christian painter was naturally solicited: *The Assumption of the Virgin*, now adorning a side chapel, counts among the memorable fruits of the painter's timely visit to his native land. This northern journey was extended as far as Düsseldorf, a sequestered town already growing illustrious for its school of religious painting. Wilhelm Schadow, co-partner in Roman labours, had here, as Director of the Academy, gathered round him devoted scholars, and Overbeck greeted his old friend as a missionary in the common cause. After receiving on all hands respectful adulations which would have turned a vainer head, the traveller bent his steps southwards, and reached Italy by way of Strasburg and Switzerland. On reaching Rome, he writes on the 1st of December to Cornelius in characteristic tone: "You will understand with what lively joy I once more saw my beloved Rome; I therefore will not conceal the painful impression which the distracted opinions and doctrines in the Fatherland have left in my mind, but I feel rest in the persuasion that, through the dispensation of Providence, my lot has been cast in this Roman seclusion, not that I intend to lay my hands idly in my lap, but, on the contrary, I shall endeavour to work with my utmost ability, spurred on all the more by the thought that even here at a distance I shall move in your circle." Assuredly as to professional prospects the passage of the Alps had extended the artist's circuit: the Italian works which chiefly mark the painter's first period had come to an end; henceforth Overbeck's labours, though prosecuted within the Roman studio, were for the good of Germany.

Overbeck, in September, 1833, witnessed an event memorable in the history of art: he was present at the opening of Raphael's tomb in the Pantheon, and a few days after he wrote to his friend Veit at Frankfort a circumstantial account, as some relief to his overwhelming emotions. The letter is here of interest as evidence of Overbeck's unshaken allegiance to the great master; if called by others a pre-Raphaelite, he remained at heart faithful to the painter from whom indeed he borrowed largely. Unlike certain of our English artists and critics, he never decried Raphael. He writes: "Know, then, I was present at the opening of Raphael's grave, and have looked upon the true and incomparable master. What a shudder came over me when the remains of the honoured painter were laid open, thou canst better conceive than I can describe. May this deep experience not be without good results for us: may the remembrance of the honoured one make us more worthy inheritors of his spirit!"[7]

Overbeck about this time, in letters to Emilie Linder, begins to express ultra views, to the prejudice of his art. He pleads that certain Biblical drawings may have for her more worth because the religious meaning dominates over the art skill. In like manner he writes apologetically concerning *The Death of St. Joseph*. The picture, he urges, embodies not so much a historic fact as an idea, the intent being not to lead the spectator to the real, but to something beyond. The purist painter then proceeds to express his invincible reluctance to study the subject from the side of life; models he had carefully avoided, because he feared that a single glance at nature would destroy the whole conception. It is with sincere regret that I have to record so pernicious a doctrine. Surely the artist's special function must always be to find out the divine element in nature, and fatal is the day when first he calls into question the essential oneness between Nature and God. But Overbeck's peculiar phase of Catholicism marred as well as made his art. Through the Church he entered a holy, heavenly sphere, and his pictures verily stand forth as the revelation of his soul. But the sublimest of doctrines sometimes prove to be utterly unpaintable, and certainly the tenets to which Overbeck gave a super-sensuous turn, in the end perplexed and clouded his art. Outraged nature took her revenge, and the sequel shows that Overbeck so diverted his vision and narrowed his pictorial range that his art fell short of the largeness of nature and humanity.

Northern Germany claimed the illustrious painter as her son, and so fitly came commissions from Cologne, Lübeck, and Hamburg. For the great Hospital in this last commercial town was painted the large oil-picture, *Christ's Agony in the Garden*. This impressive composition represents the Saviour kneeling; the head is bowed in anguish, the hands are raised in ecstasy; below, the three disciples lie asleep, and in the glory of the upper sky amid rolling clouds appears as a vision the angel bearing the cross. I paid a visit to Hamburg in order to judge of a work of which I could find but slight mention. Its characteristics are just what might have been anticipated. The drawing is studious, the expression intense, the execution feeble; in short, the technique becomes wholly subordinate to the intention. The conception has Giottesque simplicity: the shade of night brings solemnity, and the longer I stood before the canvas the more I became impressed with the quietude and fervour of the scene.[8]

We find an epitome of Overbeck's mind and art in a lovely composition, *Lo Sposalizio*. Count Raczynski had as far back as 1819 given a general commission, and at first was proposed as a subject the *Sibyl*, for which the drawing in sepia, dated 1821, now hangs in the

Count's Gallery in Berlin. The figure, pensive and poetic, resembles a mediæval Saint rather than a Sibyl. The painter afterwards found a more congenial theme in *The Marriage of the Virgin*. The treatment is wholly traditional, the style austerely pre-Raphaelite; the only expletive in the way of an idea comes with attendant angels, lyres in hand. The work was not delivered till 1836, in the meanwhile the first fire had died out, and nature was thrust into the distance. The technique had not improved, the material clothing becomes subject to the mental conception, thus are eschewed *chic* of touch and surface texture. The colour is indescribable: it pertains neither to earth nor to heaven, and yet it has more of dull clay than of iridescent light. What a misfortune that the gem-like lustre of the early Italians escaped this modern disciple! A thoroughly characteristic letter accompanied the picture. Overbeck having shut himself out from the world, seeks for his creations a like seclusion. He writes to Raczynski: "As you are wishing to send my picture to the public exhibition in Berlin, I cannot refrain from expressing my anxiety. Paintings of this kind appear to me not fitted to be seen by the motley multitude usually gathered together in exhibitions. The general public are almost sure to measure wrongly works like this, for as the eye is attracted to outward means and is engaged on technical splendours, pictures in which these qualities are held in subordination to higher aims cannot but sink into the shade. The spectator is not in the mood to honour a spiritual subject which has been thought out from a spiritual side. The place in which this picture should be seen is a chapel, or some such peaceful spot removed from disturbing surroundings."[9]

I now wish to direct the reader's attention to *The Triumph of Religion in the Arts*, otherwise *The Magnificat of Art*, or *The Christian Parnassus*, or the triumph of Mariolatry. This large and elaborate composition embodied the artist's best thoughts for ten years in the prime of life, from 1831 to 1840. Accompanying the work was a written explanation, which comprises a confession of Overbeck's art faith.[10] The Madonna, with the Infant in her arms, sits enthroned in the upper half of the canvas, and around, in mid-heaven, are ranged prophets, evangelists, and saints. On the earth below stand some sixty painters, sculptors, and architects; the heads as far as possible are taken from authentic portraits. In the midst is a fountain, the upper waters rising into the sky, the lower falling into two basins beneath. The painter explains his meaning as follows: "The fountain in the centre is the emblem of the well of water springing up into eternal life, thus denoting the heavenward direction of Christian Art as opposed to the idea of the ancients, who represented the stream as flowing downwards from Mount Parnassus. Every manifestation of art therefore is honoured so far only as it looks towards heaven. The fountain descends into two mirrors: the upper one reflects heaven, the lower receives earthly objects; thus is indicated the twofold character of art, which, on the one hand, in its spiritual essence comes with every good thought from above, and which, on the other, is derived from the outward forms of nature. This twofold sphere of art is signified by the position assigned to the assembled artists in relation to the two mirrors of water." Overbeck next proceeds to expound his pictorial judgments. He gives Raphael a white robe as symbolic of universal genius, "for as white light contains the seven prismatic colours, so does Raphael's art unite all the qualities we gaze on with wonder." Michelangelo sits apart on a fragment of antique sculpture, his back turned alike on the Fountain and the Madonna. I once ventured to ask Overbeck in his studio for some explanation of this harsh judgment; he calmly but firmly replied that he thought the verdict according to the evidence. Still less mercy is shown to the Venetians, and as for Correggio, he is stigmatised as utterly lost. On the other hand, Fra Angelico, the Tuscan School, Dürer, and the brothers Van Eyck receive due reverence. But it has fairly been questioned whether the majority of the sixty or more artists here immortalised would thank the painter for his pains. The reading given to historic facts is narrow, partial, not to say perverted, and could content only such ultra critics as Rio, Montalembert, and Pugin. *The Triumph of Religion* [11] I have known for more than a quarter of a century, and have heard much of its profundity, spiritualism, and symbolism. But no critic will assign to the picture the first rank among works of creative reason and imagination; the comparison has inevitably been instituted with Raphael's *Disputa*, in the Vatican, to which it is confessedly inferior. Historically, it finds a place sufficiently honourable by the side of Francia and Pinturicchio. Its avowed merits are considerable; its very scale and the vastness of the labour give importance; the canvas extends to a breadth and height of about fifteen feet. The composition, if not bold or masterly, is careful and thoughtful, the drawing scholastic; the heads are wrought as biographic studies, the draperies cast into balanced harmonies. The execution is steady, without show or fling; the colour, as always, is the reverse of alluring: Venetian splendours are eschewed in favour of pigments thin, dull, and crude. Yet the technique has usual soundness; the materials stand firm and unchanged. The picture has the advantage of a commanding position in the handsome new gallery in Frankfort, and, notwithstanding its defects and shortcomings, must be accounted as among the most memorable achievements of the century.

Overbeck made *The Triumph of Religion* a propaganda of his pictorial faith, and wrote his explanatory text for the special benefit of young painters. The document concludes with the following emphatic and affectionate appeal: "And now, my dear young friend and brother artist, so ardently striving to excel in the Fine Arts, I have placed a picture before you in which you may wander as in a garden. Here you see all the great masters: behold how the future lies spread before you, like the bright distance in this picture, so that you may be encouraged thereby in your noble task. Strive to approach the great masters with all the powers of your mind, but know that you can only reach their eminence by steadily keeping in view the goal which I have endeavoured in this painting to place before you. Several of the artists here assembled may serve as warnings to you: the Venetians went astray as soon as they made colouring the principal object of attraction, and so by degrees they sank in sensuality. The effeminate Correggio proceeded in this career at a more rapid rate, until he had cast aside every restraint of modesty and morality, and gave himself up to unbridled voluptuousness.[12] Michael Angelo set up the antique as an object of idolatry, and Raphael was tempted to taste the forbidden fruit, and so the sin of apostasy in the fine arts became manifest. In after times, indeed, various attempts have been made to elevate the arts; but as no remedy was applied to the source of the evil, the result proved on the whole unsuccessful. This is also the reason why none of the celebrated masters of late times have been introduced into our painting.[13] In conclusion, you may unhesitatingly adopt as a principle that the fine arts can alone be beneficial to man when, like the wise virgins, they go out to meet the bridegroom in humility and modesty, with their lamps burning and fed with the faith and the fear of God: only as such daughters of heaven are they worthy of your love."

Ten years of the painter's later period, reaching from 1843 to 1852, were dedicated to the Life of Christ as recorded by the four Evangelists. German artists of the modern time have revived the practice of the old religious painters of composing Biblical series, and such a narrative is technically termed a "cyclus." Overbeck evolved three such consecutive compositions—"The Gospels" in forty cartoons, "The Sacraments" in seven, and "The Stations" in fourteen. The large drawings for "The Gospels" or "Evangelists"[14] I was accustomed to see from time to time while in progress within the studio; none were ever carried out, as the artist might have hoped, in oils, or as wall pictures or tapestries, but all, in common with most of his drawings, have been widely diffused by means of engraving.[15] Overbeck was specially qualified by his habits of mind and literary tastes and antecedents thus to write off his thoughts in outline; his drawings may be compared to "thinking aloud," and one scene after another reads as consecutive sonnets bearing on continuous themes. The events depicted as a matter of course fall into accustomed routine; they almost of necessity begin with *The Annunciation* and end with *The Ascension*. Yet Overbeck, while inspired was not enslaved by his predecessors; often are presented novel and even bold conceptions, as in *The Massacre of the Innocents* (1843) and *Barabbas released and borne in Triumph* (1849). Such designs prove an intellect neither

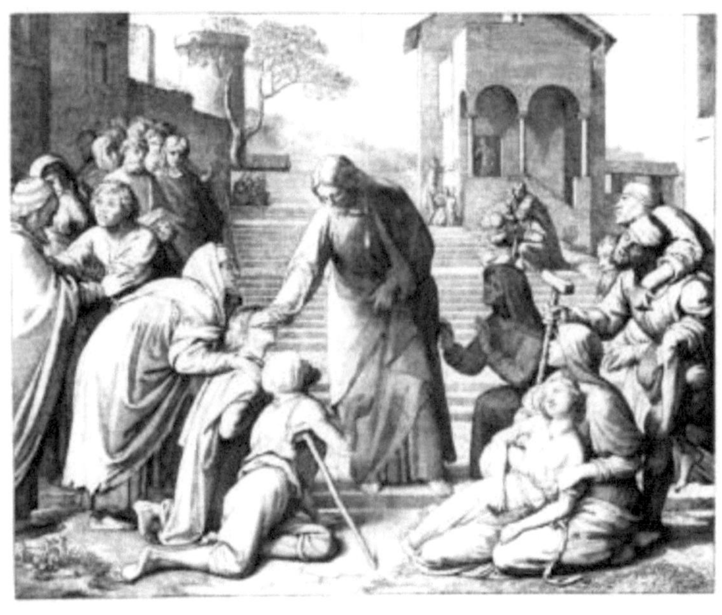

CHRIST HEALING THE SICK

servile nor sterile. Certain other compositions are marred by affectation and sentimentality, traits of morbid moods increasing with years, and which contrast strangely with the healthiness and robustness of the great old masters. Fitly have been chosen to illustrate these pages *The Naming of St. John* (1843), *Christ Healing the Sick* (1843), *Christ's Entry into Jerusalem* (1849), *The Entombment* (1844), and *The Resurrection* (1848). Two other illustrations, *Christ in the Temple* and Christ *falling under the Cross* show variations on the Gospel series. Overbeck may be compared to certain fastidious writers who mature by endless emendations and finishing touches; he loved to recur oft and again to favourite texts, changing attitudes, adding or subtracting figures, episodes, or accessories. His lifelong compositions are as a peopled world of the elect and precious: many of the characters we claim as old acquaintances; the figures come, go, and return again, changed, yet without a break in personal identity. They move round a common centre; Christ is their life; they are in soul and body Christian.

These "Gospels" have taken a permanent place in the world's Christian Art. If not wholly worthy of so large and grand a theme, they yet scarcely suffer from comparison with like efforts by other artists. They have hardly less of unction and holiness than Fra Angelico's designs, while undoubtedly they display profounder science and art. That they have nothing in common with the Bible of Gustave Doré is much to their praise; on the other hand, that they lack the inventive fertility and the imaginative flight of the Bible of Julius Schnorr indicates that they fall short of universality. These Gospels, it may also be said, pertain not to the Church militant, but to the Church triumphant; not to the world at large, but to a select company of believers. They teach the passive virtues—patience, resignation, long-suffering, and so far realise the painter's ideal of earth as the portal to heaven. Certain spheres were beyond his ken. The marriage of Cana did not for him flow with the wine of gladness; he had no fellowship with the nuptial banquet as painted by Veronese. His pencil shunned the Song of Miriam and the Dance of the Daughter of Herodias; it could not pass, like the pen of England's epic poet, with a light fantastic touch from "Il Penseroso" to "L'Allegro;" his walk was narrow as a convent cloister; his art was attuned to the sound of the vesper bell.

Overbeck's modes of study and habits of work were like himself—secluded and self-contained. His strength did not permit prolonged labour, and his mind was easily put out of tune; yet by method and strict economy of time he was able, as we have seen, to get through a very considerable amount of work. Each day had its allotted task. He rose summer and winter between five and six o'clock, and usually went to church; at seven he took a simple breakfast, then entered his studio and worked on till one. This was the hour for dinner, a frugal meal preceded by the customary grace. After a little repose, action was resumed about half-past two, and continued till four, or sometimes even to six. Then came exercise, mostly a meditative walk; in early times, before the habits of a recluse had grown confirmed, the painter enjoyed an evening's stroll with choice spirits, such as Niebuhr and Bunsen, but in later years he preferred his own communings, his thoughts turning upon art or finding diversion only among the beauties of nature. Within the house he became abstracted; he wandered about lost to outward surroundings, and would brook no interruption. In the winter evenings, at least in later life, he relaxed so far as to join in some table game; but his hours were early, he supped at eight, then retired to his room for meditation, and was always in bed by ten. General family prayers were not the order of the household; the constant habit was individual devotion in private. The Pope took a fatherly care over the pious artist, and granted him privileges permitted only to the few. And Overbeck was on his part strict and zealous in all Church functions, and neglected no means of building up the Christian life. Each day in fact was so nicely apportioned between religion and art, that the morning and the evening worship blended indissolubly with the midday work.

The bodily and mental aspect of Overbeck is well known. I myself had the privilege of first seeing the painter when in the Cenci Palace, as far back as the year 1848. My journal describes a man impressive in presence, tall and attenuated in body, worn by ill-health and suffering, the face emaciated and tied round by a piece of black silk. The mind had eaten into the flesh; the features were sorrow-laden. The voice sank into whispers, the words were plaintive and sparse; noiselessly the artist glided among easels bearing pictorial forms austere as his own person, meekly he offered explanations of works which embodied his very soul, timidly sought retreat and passed as a shadow by — the emblem of an art given in answer to prayer and pertaining to two worlds.

The painter, as drawn or described by himself and others, presents an interesting psychological study: no historic portrait reveals closer correspondence between the inner and the outer man. Cornelius delineated his friend at the age of twenty-three: the type is ascetic and æsthetic after the pre-Raphaelite pattern affected by the Nazarites. Führich, one of the fraternity, describes his first impressions: on entering the studio he beheld a tall, spare figure, noble in head, the hair flowing over smooth temples to the shoulders, the forehead reflective, the calm eye "soul-full," the whole aspect that of "inner living." It is added, "at once I felt a soul fulfilment." Yet another artist-disciple, Edwin Speckter,[16] also leaves a graphic record penned in 1831 as follows: "A melancholy and heart-moving impression has Overbeck made upon me: I beheld a tall, spare man, with thin, light hair, shadowed by a black cap, whose eyes looked forth sadly, as with an expression of unutterable suffering. His mouth contracted at each word into a forced yet sweet smile. He looked just as a timid prisoner, who dreads in every corner to see a spy. Yet in all his speech and ways appeared wondrous humility, modesty, and kindly geniality, which, however, did not attract, but in a strange manner repelled. I hardly dared to open my mouth, and only spoke softly and by way of inquiry. Freely to impart my mind as with others was impossible. My breast felt oppressed, and truly I scarcely knew what to say when he unceasingly begged pardon that he should dare to show his works: he called them 'insignificant,' 'nothing,' esteemed himself fortunate that people should choose to give commissions to so unworthy an individual, only he pitied the patrons that they had not fallen on a more capable man. And then when I asked if I might come again, he replied, 'Good heavens! if I would give myself the trouble, he should be only too delighted.' I could almost have laughed, but with tears in my eyes."

FOOTNOTES:

[1] For further particulars as to Overbeck's wife, "Nina," see 'Erinnerungen und Leben der Malerin Louise Seidler,' Berlin, Verlag von Wilhelm Hertz, 1875. According to this authority the young lady was the illegitimate daughter of a gentleman of aristocratic family in Vienna, from whom she received a dowry. She had come to Rome in search of health, and possessing talents, accomplishments and charms, and being withal a "fanatic Catholic," she won the affections of the impressible painter. "The young couple," we are told, passed "a soul-satisfying" honeymoon, and took up their abode in the Villa Palombara, near the Baths of Diocletian. In the private collection of Herr Bockenheimer, Frankfort, I have found an exquis-

ite drawing, wherein the artist is said to have depicted himself, his wife, and two children.

[2] Mrs. Jameson, in 'The Legends of the Monastic Orders,' illustrates the visions and ecstasies of St. Francis from the pictures of Giotto and others down to Domenichino. Coming to our times, the only work found worthy of such companionship is that of Overbeck. The modern German does not suffer by comparison with the old Italian masters. The fresco was finished 1830; shortly after, an earthquake visited the spot and destroyed a large portion of the church, but *The Vision of St. Francis* remained intact. The cartoon for the picture is in the Library, Lübeck, framed, hung, but badly seen. I examined and noted it October 1880. It is in chalk, on paper mounted on canvas; the form is lunette, the base about 20 feet broad; the figures are life-size. The heads, hands and draperies are thoroughly studied in a broad, large manner. The work when exhibited in Munich in 1831, on the artist's visit to Germany, obtained high commendation. The oil study made for the colour is now in the Leipzig Museum: measurement, 2 feet 3 inches by 2 feet 7 inches. The cartoon has been lithographed by Koch: the fresco itself is photographed.

[3] Portrait of *Vittoria Caldoni*, oil, on canvas, nearly life-size, about 3 feet by 2 feet. *Holy Family*, about 4 feet 6 inches by 3 feet: oil, on rough Roman canvas, signed "F. O. 1825": better colour than usual: in good condition, but, like many pictures in the New Pinakothek, revived by the Pettenkofer process: the beautiful engraving by Felsing has a sale quite unusual for Overbeck. "Italia und Germania," about 3 feet 5 inches by 2 feet 9 inches, oil, on canvas: manner hard and dry: lithographed by F. Piloty.

[4] See 'Historisch-Politische Blätter für das Katholische Deutschland,' before quoted.

[5] *The Death of St. Joseph*, oil, on canvas, 3 feet by 2 feet 3 inches, was at last completed 1836, and appeared two years later in the Munich Exhibition: the price was less than 100*l*. A small drawing for the picture was, with others in the possession of Emilie Linder, lithographed for devotional purposes: the lady with characteristic generosity sent the proceeds of publication to the painter. On her death in 1867 her collection went by bequest to the Basle Museum, where

are conserved, besides *The Death of St. Joseph,* ten drawings in pencil. Among the last are *God appearing to Elias on Mount Horeb, The Finding of Moses, The Israelites gathering Manna, The Madonna and St. Joseph worshipping the Infant Jesus, Christ found in the Temple,* and *The Awakening of Jairus's Daughter.* Of the last I have met with two other examples. The engraving, *Christ in the Temple,* illustrating this volume, is from the drawing in this collection.

[6] The principal drawings at Stift Neuburg have been mentioned in previous pages. I will now add from notes taken on the spot: Portrait of Cornelius by Overbeck and a companion portrait on the same paper of Overbeck by Cornelius. Pencil: 1 foot 4 inches by 1 foot 3 inches. This joint handiwork, presented to their friend on the eve of his leaving Rome for Germany, bears the following inscription: "In Remembrance of our friend C. F. Schlosser, from F. Overbeck and J. P. Cornelius. Rome, 16 March, 1812." The latest drawing in the collection, date 1836, represents Christ bearing the Lamb: the Saviour opens His mantle and shows a flaming heart. This is one of the first signs of the painter's ultimate tendency to exalt dogmas and legends at the expense of essential truth and beauty. Some of the chief drawings at Stift Neuburg have been published in photography by Bruckmann, Munich.

[7] Overbeck's letter on the opening of the tomb in the Pantheon is published in Passavant's 'Life of Raphael.'

[8] *Christ's Agony in the Garden* is on canvas, 7 feet wide by 11 feet high: figures size of life: without signature or date: the manner is that of the middle period: the year I believe to be between 1831 and 1835. The system of colour, though not without the depth and solemnity of the early schools of Lombardy, is that peculiar to the religious art of modern Germany: it is dull, heavy and opaque. I would quote as an interesting proof of nature-study, still maintained at this pronounced period, a foreground plant and flower exquisitely drawn and affectionately painted. The picture is seen to utmost disadvantage: the cold and poverty-stricken surroundings are those usually deemed appropriate in Lutheran Germany.

[9] The present position of *The Marriage of the Virgin* in the Raczynski Gallery, Berlin, has just those "disturbing surroundings" which the painter dreaded. It is crowded among discordant works,

and is hung so high that I had to ask for a ladder to examine its quality and condition. The oil pigments remain sound save some small surface cracks. The size is about 6 feet by 4 feet. The modest price paid by the munificent patron, and for which he received the artist's grateful acknowledgments, was somewhat under 100*l.* sterling. Surely Overbeck did not paint for filthy lucre.

[10] See account of 'Religion glorified by the Fine Arts,' written by the painter himself and translated by Mr. John Macray: published by Ryman, Oxford; 2nd edition, 1850.

[11] The picture has been engraved by Amsler, and is also photographed. The cartoon is in the Carlsruhe Gallery, framed and hung: it measures about 12 feet wide by 14 feet high: it is in charcoal or chalk, on squares of whity-brown paper mounted on canvas. This drawing is remarkable for thoroughness in form and character; indeed, it is just what a cartoon should be. Countless preliminary studies of separate figures and draperies must have preceded it. Overbeck in a letter, 28th December, 1839, to Emilie Linder mentions three cartoons or studies. One large one being the above. A second smaller, 4 feet 8 inches square, in sepia, on canvas. This I examined October, 1880, in the National Gallery, Berlin: the execution in parts is poor. The work had been sent for sale, but was not purchased. The third sketch is described by the artist as different in proportions and composition. It is in black chalk and pencil on red paper. The painter names £100 as the price: he received £1300 for the picture.

[12] Surely Overbeck is unjust to the masterpieces of Correggio in Parma and Dresden, including two Holy Families, *Il Giorno* and *La Notte*. He likewise must have forgotten Titian's religious pictures in Venice and Vienna, *The Assumption* and sundry Holy Families. The "young artist" has to remember that a picture is different from a homily: that art has to be valued for her own sake, that drawing, composition, light, shade and colour are indispensable elements in every art work. Overbeck shirks the stern truth that the first duty of a painter is to paint.

[13] It is difficult to remain tolerant of such intolerance. Why does not Overbeck declare plainly that Ary Scheffer is excluded because he was a Protestant? As spectators a place in the picture is assigned

to Cornelius, Veit, and to Overbeck himself, all Roman Catholics, whilst Schnorr, as a Protestant, is deemed unworthy to appear. It is interesting to observe that Overbeck's darling son is introduced in the character of a young Englishman.

[14] The cartoons for the Gospels, originally made for an art dealer in Prague, were afterwards acquired by the late Baron Lotzbeck of Weihern, near Munich, and are now in the possession of the son, the present Baron: they are framed and protected under glass.

[15] See 'L'Évangile Illustré: Quarante Compositions de Fréderic Overbeck: gravées par les meilleurs Artistes de l'Allemagne:' Schulgen, Düsseldorf and Paris. Overbeck had an aversion to the heavy and mechanical schools of engraving; he objected to meaningless masses of shadow and to the multiplication of lines inexpressive of form. Accordingly these engravings from the Gospels, in common with other plates from the master, possess merits the opposites to such defects. Like the original drawings, they are chiefly dependent on outline, and even their slightness is not without the advantage of suggestiveness. Four illustrations here are facsimiles of the engravings.

[16] See 'Briefe eines deutschen Künstlers aus Italien, aus den nachgelassenen Papieren von Edwin Speckter.' Leipzig: Brockhaus, 1846. Also see 'Bunte Blätter, von A. W. Ambros.' Leipzig: Leuckart, 1872.

CHAPTER IV.

LATE WORKS — CONCLUSION — THE PAINTER AND HIS ART.

OVERBECK, as we have seen, deliberately laid out his life for tranquillity; but not sheltered, as Fra Angelico, in a cloister, his serene mind was at times clouded by trouble. First came the death of his son, then he lost a brother, and afterwards was bereaved of his wife. All accounts tell that the darling son, Alfons Maria, inherited the rare gifts of the father, and unhappily also was a sharer in like bodily frailty. He had been reared with tenderest solicitude, in the hope that he might carry on the good work. The profession chosen was that of architecture, an art which the Christian painter felt to be of a "mystic nature," being something "musical," and "the visible emblem of religious enthusiasm." But the bright promise was soon darkened: the youth died in the autumn of 1840, at the early age of eighteen. The father in overwhelming sorrow recounts, in a letter to Emilie Linder, how he had watched over the sick bed, and had snatched up a pencil by the quarter of an hour to assuage his grief. The boy was dutiful, and filled with filial love—he was so good that the people called him a saint. The stricken parent turned to art as "a crutch to support his lameness, and as a solace to his tears."

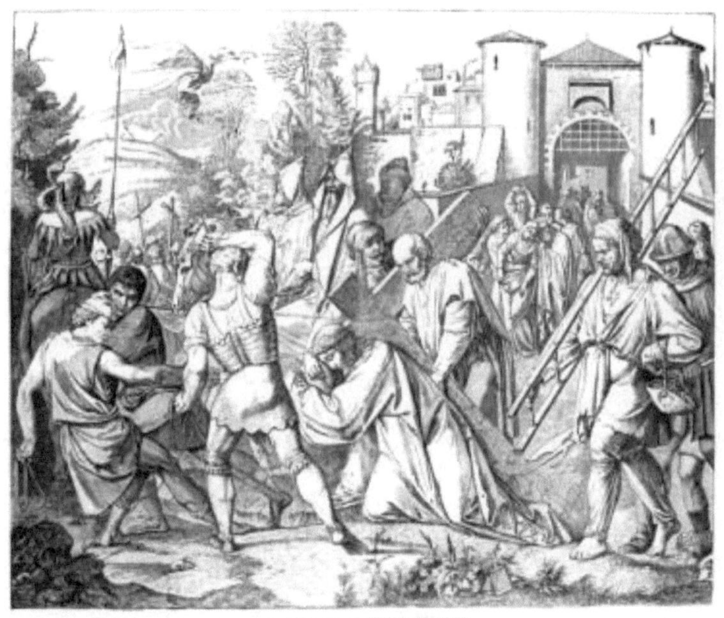

CHRIST FALLING UNDER THE CROSS.
(From a Drawing in the Picture Print Room.)

The picture of *The Entombment*, or rather *The Pietà*, in Lübeck, tells of the mind's heavy burden. In 1837 an association had been formed, and money subscribed among friends and admirers, who desired that the native city should possess some work worthy of the painter's renown. In 1842, on the completion of the first sketch and the cartoon, a letter arrived in Lübeck, saying that the grief through which the artist had passed was thrown into a composition that expressed the uttermost anguish of the soul. And again, in 1846, on the completion of the work, the Christian man writes, praying that this "lamentation over the death of the Son of God may arouse in the spectator true faith and repentance. May this painting, begun in tears for my own and only son, and finished in grief for the loss of my dear brother, draw tears from the eyes of Him who shed not only tears, but blood, in order that His death might be our life. Such aim have I always in my art, without which it would seem idle, indeed blasphemous."

The Pietà [1] was exhibited in Rome, and friendly criticisms were followed by final touches, with the filial intent to make a worthy offering to the parental city. In March, 1846, Overbeck announces, in the most modest terms, that the labour of love had at length been dispatched to Lübeck, and, much to his joy, a quiet side chapel of the choir of the Marien Kirche was chosen for its resting-place. The impression on entering this secluded spot, shut in by a locked gate, is almost startling; the eye gazes, as it were, on the actual scene: the figures are life-size; the pictorial style is, perhaps, all the more persuasive because it belongs to a remote time—nothing modern breaks the spell of sacred associations. The spectator is transported to a sphere super-mundane, and altogether religious. The dead Christ, well modelled and a fine piece of flesh painting, lies stretched on the ground in a white winding-sheet, and, as sometimes with the old painters, the body seems not dead but sleeping, as if expectant of resurrection. The composition is strictly traditional, indeed the *Pietà* of Perugino in the Pitti Palace has been implicitly followed: around are the holy women weeping, with disciples and Nicodemus and Joseph of Arimathæa. Every head, hand, and drapery, are thoroughly studied. Dark rocks, lofty cypresses, and distant hills, make up a landscape which adds solemnity and depth of colour. Within a few minutes' walk of the Marien Kirche and this *Pietà* still remains Memling's masterpiece, which, as already related, had deeply impressed the youthful painter while yet in the Lübeck home, but allegiance had been long, we know, transferred from old German to Italian art, and accordingly the style adopted recalls well-remembered compositions by Francia, Fra Bartolommeo, and Perugino. Not a single new motive intrudes; in fact, Overbeck no more desired a new art than a new religion; for him the old remained unchangeably true,—sacred characters were handed down immutably as by apostolic succession; he would rearrange an attitude, but feared to lose personal identity; he desired that this *Pietà* should awaken such holy associations as environ old pictures.

Overbeck received a commission from a Yorkshire squire, Mr. Rhodes, to paint an altar-piece for the Protestant church of St. Thomas, in Leeds, recently built from the design of Mr. Butterfield.

Naturally the Incredulity of the Apostle was chosen as the subject, and the picture[2] reached completion in 1851. The composition is in no way out of keeping with the Anglican Church; it is without taint of Romanism; but we are told by Ernst Förster, the Munich critic,[3] that "people were not well pleased with the work," at all events it never reached its destined place. Mr. Rhodes had brought the picture to England from Overbeck's studio, and being for disposal, it was offered to Mr. Beresford Hope, who gladly became the owner, at the price of 300*l.*, the modest sum asked by the artist. The scene is thrown upon canvas with the painter's habitual simplicity, brevity, and breadth. Christ in commanding, yet benignant, attitude, with arm uplifted, utters the words: "Reach hither thy hand and thrust it into my side, and be not faithless, but believing." The Apostle reverently approaches. Beyond stretches a distant landscape with a mountain-height that might be mistaken for the crested summit of Soracte. The lines of composition flow symmetrically, the sentiment has quiet dignity, with that sense of the divine presence which seldom fails the painter. The picture hangs in the drawing-room of Mr. Hope's town-house, and, though painted for a church, conforms to domestic uses, not being "too bright or good for human nature's daily food." The personation of the Saviour when once seen will not be forgotten; the figure, indeed, was cherished by the artist, for the motive with slight variation is repeated in *The Vocation of the Apostles James and John* (*see* Illustration), and again in *The Sacrament of Marriage*. Overbeck had none of the modern unrest which seeks novelty for its own sake; as a Christian artist, his growth was that of grace; and, if tested here and elsewhere by the worthiness of his conception of the God-Man, no painter attained a more heavenly ideal. It is hard to realise on earth a more perfect divinity than seen in the design *Feed my Sheep*. *The Incredulity of St. Thomas* has been exhibited in England twice; first in 1853, in the Royal Academy, where, I remember, it was honoured with a conspicuous place in the large room; afterwards, in 1857, it was seen in the Manchester Art Treasures. As far as I know, it is the only large and important work of the master submitted to the English public.

Overbeck, thirteen years after the death of his son, was in 1853 bereft of his wife, who had been his companion and caretaker for more than thirty years. She died suddenly, yet, as her husband thankfully records, with all the consolations the soul could desire. She had in the morning been to church and taken the sacrament; she was then seized with difficulty of breathing, but, on reaching home, revived, and raised her voice to the praise and glory of God; after, she grew worse, desired to see the priest, received extreme unction, and so died.

The good painter, when the help-mate of his life was taken away, felt utterly desolate and disabled. He had never been accustomed to look after the house; some thirty poor families are said to have been dependent on his bounty; but as for himself he took little thought, and all he desired was to be saved from mundane cares. In Rome there happened to be a certain family of Hoffmanns, who, like the painter, had forsaken Protestantism for Catholicism. They were endowed with the worldly faculties in which the Christian artist was wanting, and so a close relationship had conveniently grown up. Overbeck, on the death of his wife, being absolutely incapable of getting on alone, arranged to live with this family; moreover, he adopted Madame Hoffmann, a lady of forty, as his daughter, and the adoption included the husband and the children. They seem to have made him comfortable, and letters exist which give expression to his gratitude. They, on their side, reaped their reward, inasmuch as on the death of the good artist they came into the possession of the contents of his studio, his papers, and correspondence, moneys, and all other properties. After the aforesaid family arrangement, the blood relations found little favour, and all who bore the name of Overbeck were cut off without a shilling.

Earthly trouble did but turn the painter's gaze heavenwards, and his art, which in time of trial came as consolation, grew all the more spiritual as it passed through waters of affliction. Few painters, even in the good old days, obtained so sympathetic a public. Belief in a mission begat like faith in others, and so solicitations came for drawings and pictures far in excess of available time and strength. Certain commissions could not be entertained, secular subjects had been long eschewed, religion and the Church were alone accounted worthy of service. Therefore, in genial mood, was the great picture for Cologne Cathedral undertaken and carried out. The work occupied no less than nine years; the cartoon was already in course of preparation in 1846, and the picture reached completion in 1855.

But, as with other engagements, the negotiations and preliminary correspondence extended over a longer period. Thus, as far back as 23rd August, 1829, Overbeck, while working on the Assisi fresco, writes from Santa Maria degli Angeli to his friend Mosler, stating that the Düsseldorf Kunst-Verein wish for some picture; but prior engagements stand in the way: he foresees that on the return to Rome he will find his studio crowded with works begun, but still unfinished, besides sketches of all sorts and sizes for pictures not even commenced. He therefore asks for delay, and ends with apologies for not writing more on the parental plea that "though it is Sunday, I have long given my promise to my boy Alfons, whose tenth birthday is to-day, that he shall have a ride on a donkey, and I am all the more obliged to keep my word because my fresco work here compels me for the moment to neglect him. We are all, thank God, very well, and enjoy a thousand blessings in this abode of Paradise." Three months later he writes under mistaken impressions as to the character of the commission; he wishes to know the architectural style of the church, and hopes it may be Gothic; he desires accurate measurements, because the picture must appear to belong to its destined place, and then ends in the following characteristic terms: "I repeat once more that the commission fills me with utmost pleasure, but to you I must confide my great anxiety, that I fear this picture is destined for a Protestant church, as I hear it is to be for some newly-built church. Should this, indeed, be the case, then pray try to give the whole thing another direction, as such a commission would not suit me at all, and to refuse it would be very disagreeable to me."

Overbeck's visit to Cologne, in 1831, naturally led to further conferences concerning the picture for the Cathedral. The proposal, at first, was that a triptych on a gold ground, in a Gothic frame, should be painted for the high altar. Drawings were prepared, the general scheme was approved by Cornelius, and the Archbishop gave his assent. But objections having been raised on historic or archæologic grounds, the pictorial reredos was abandoned in favour of the present stone altar table. The artist felt deeply disappointed, and craved the prayers of his friend Steinle, who was engaged on the decoration of the choir. Fortunately, the services of Overbeck were only transferred from the high altar to the Madonna chapel, renovated to receive *The Assumption* commissioned to be painted. The cartoon was prepared and approved, and while engaged on the work the artist expressed himself supremely happy; he had no higher ambition than to be found worthy of a place in the great Cathedral.

The Assumption of the Madonna [4] is suited to its surroundings; it is in keeping with the Gothic structure and decorations, and in companionship with old triptychs and other works which carry the mind back to remote ages. The composition stands forth as a vision of the imagination; from the darkness of the grave into the light of the upper sky rises the Queen of Heaven, borne upwards on angels' wings; midway sustained by clouds are the adoring host, comprising Adam, Eve, Abraham, and King David; on the ground below are seen, in miniature, the disciples around the empty tomb. The whole conception is in perfect accord with the rites and ceremonies of the Church; while looking at the picture and listening to the voices in the choir, the harmonies between form and sound seem fitly attuned.

Overbeck, on the completion of the Cologne picture, revisited Germany for the second and last time. On the 20th July, 1855, he left Rome, proceeded to Florence, thence by way of Switzerland reached Frankfort, and extended his journey as far as Düsseldorf. In Cologne he stayed some weeks, and a festival, with usual laudatory speeches, was given in his honour. I happened to encounter the painter during his sojourn; I could hardly believe my eyes when I discovered the venerable artist gazing with accustomed placidity at Rubens's brutal representation of *The Crucifixion of St. Peter*, head downwards. With reverence I approached the great master, and received a kindly shake of the hand. Overbeck on the return-journey passed a quiet month at Mayence; he also once more saw his old friends at Stift Neuburg, near Heidelberg. In Frankfort many sympathetic hours were spent with his attached companion Steinle, whose elevated works proved a renewed delight, and whose happy family circle recalled his own joys and losses. The town of Spires also received a visit, the inducement being Schraudolph's extensive frescoes, then in progress within the Cathedral. Posterity has reason to lament that these important works were not entrusted to the chief of Christian painters. Some further weeks passed pleasantly among congenial minds in Munich, but friends were grieved to mark growing infirmities. Overbeck had reached the age of sixty-six, and Emilie Linder writes sorrowfully, that he was the only person over whose death she could rejoice, because all pertaining to the body had become a painful burden. Even the affectionate demonstrations of his countrymen were too much for him, and so gladly he turned his steps homewards. Yet not without lingering regrets did he journey southwards, and on reaching the summit of the Brenner he writes: "I turned round once more and gave, through the streams flowing northwards, a last greeting to my German land." After four months' absence, home comforts brought rest to his troubled mind.

Overbeck, after the death of his wife in 1853, left the Cenci Palace and went to dwell in the more quiet region of the Esquiline Hill, near the church of Santa Maria Maggiore. Later on he removed to the house in which he died, belonging to a convent, in the Via Porta Pia on the Quirinal Hill, near to the little church of San Bernardo, where he worshipped and lies buried. I remember the sequestered dwelling on the Esquiline, lying away from the road in one of those Italian wildernesses called a garden or a vineyard. The surroundings were inspiring; the eye wandered among churches and ruins, and beyond stretched the Roman Campagna, spanned by aqueducts and bounded by the Alban Hills, with Rocca di Papa, the painter's country retreat. The studio, which on Sundays continued to be crowded with strangers from all countries, had little in common with the ordinary run of painting rooms. Showy sketches, picturesque costumes, gay carpets and draperies, which commonly make a fashionable lounge, were wholly wanting. Like the studio of Steinle in Frankfort, all was in keeping with an art not dependent on outward materials, but reliant on inward thought. Around were ranged compositions embodying ideas, cartoons and drawings in no way decorative, but simple and austere studies of form in light and shade, or slightly tinted. At this period were thus evolved the pictorial series of the *Via Crucis* and *The Seven Sacraments*. Turning from these creations to the painter himself, the visitor might be tempted to indulge in psychological speculations touching the processes whereby the spirit of the man passed into objective shape. More and more the old and solitary master withdrew his affections from earthly concerns, he approached the close of life as the sun which sets to rise on a new day, and his art breathed the atmosphere of those pure regions where his beloved ones were at rest.

In the summer time was usually sought some country abode, not for remission of labour, but for refreshment through change of scene amid the beauties of nature. Overbeck,

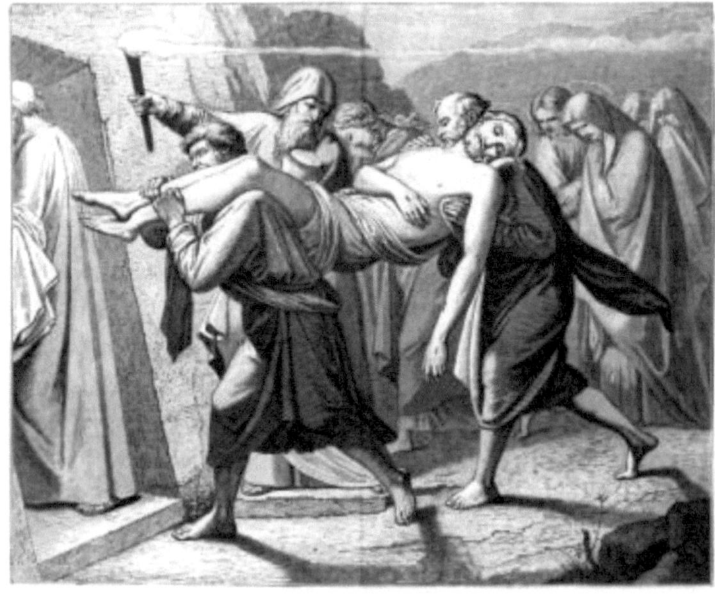

in 1856, was full of work, and in the autumn he journeyed to Perugia, and took as his travelling companions the small drawings of the *Via Crucis*. There, in the cradle of Umbrian art, in the presence of Perugino and Raphael, he carried out the scenes of *The Passion*. In the hill country of Perugia his thoughts turned to the hills round about Jerusalem, olive gardens spoke of the Garden of Gethsemane, a land lovely, yet sad, told of Him who trod the Via Dolorosa. The painter divided the day between the practice of his art, Church functions, and social intercourse; he revisited the scenes of his labours at Assisi, and rejoiced the German Sisterhood of St. Francis by a visit. The next year the picturesque district of Ariccia was chosen for summer sojourn, with the advantage of Cornelius within the distance of a walk. The following autumn the two old friends revisited the spot. Here the water-colour drawings of the *Via Crucis*, or *The Stations*, were with earnest solicitude brought to completion.

The Stations in "the history of our Lord" have been accustomed to comprise Christ's last sufferings, and in their symbolic meaning "represent the way to Calvary through which the believer is typically supposed to enter into the inner and holier part of the Church." Such compositions are almost indispensable to every Roman Catholic place of worship, however humble; therefore Overbeck, desiring that his art should at all seasons furnish aids to devotion, designed these fourteen stations on the Via Dolorosa. According to precedent, the series begins with *Jesus Condemned*, and ends with *The Entombment*. The compositions were elaborated in two forms, the one as cartoons, the other as water-colour drawings.[5] The treatment is, of course, traditional, and the general style does but suggest the line of criticism with which the reader must by this time be familiar; more than ever we here encounter sermons for the edification of the faithful rather than works appealing to the artist. The notes which a few years since I made before the drawings in the Vatican read somewhat severe, yet I ought hardly to withhold the impressions left on the mind. Utmost devotion and sincerity will be taken for granted, but I found that the excessive striving after religious feeling degenerated into morbid affectation and spiritual spasm, that sentiment passed into sentimentality, and that simplicity scarcely escaped childishness. Throughout became painfully apparent the lack of physical sinew and dramatic force; the characters, not being modelled on the life, wanted truth to nature; they were afflicted with a bodily frailty and mental infirmity wholly unequal to the tragic situation. These shortcomings in works of noblest motive may be ascribed to two causes: first, advancing age, with increasing loss of power; secondly, the confirmed habit of slighting art and ignoring nature in order to magnify some favourite dogma. Thus the divine painter in late years missed his aim and marred his work.

These reflections receive confirmation in *The Seven Sacraments*, compositions which are triumphs of faith at the expense of art. The painter, however, in fairness, must be allowed to speak for himself. "I must," he writes, "first set forth what my conception of art is. Art to me is as the harp of David, whereupon I would desire that Psalms should at all times be sounded to the praise of the Lord. For when earth and sea and everything that therein is, when Heaven and all the powers of Heaven unite in extolling their Creator, how can man fail to join with every faculty and gift his Maker has endowed him with in this universal hymn of thanksgiving? And especially how can one of the noblest attributes he possesses—the creative talent revealed in art—fail to acknowledge that its highest glory and noblest end consist in offering in art's own peculiar language Psalms and Songs of Praise to the Lord? So precisely as Psalms of Praise would I wish to be accepted my seven representations of the Sacraments, which, as so many fountains of grace, the Church causes abundantly and ceaselessly to flow. These mercies of God are the subjects of my seven pictures. As regards their style and execution, they may be compared to tapestries after the manner of the Arazzi of Raphael, such as it is customary to display in Italy on feast days for the adornment of churches, and serving for the instruction of the people in a language all can understand. Similar tapestries might, in a more favourable time than the present, have been wrought from these representations, but they appear now only as designs preparatory to their possible completion some day in fresco or tempera."[6]

Biblical history received ample exposition in numerous accessory compositions. Each of *The Seven Sacraments* was surrounded by a predella, a frieze, and two side borders. Some of these long spaces dilated into several themes, and thus the total number of subsidiary subjects falls little short of forty. The foliated and floral ornament in style is not Raphaelesque, but more allied to early Gothic; the manner is graceful but feeble. The scheme embodies types in the Old Testament with their fulfilment in the New; both conjoined are brought to bear on the teachings of the Church concerning the Sacraments. Some of the analogies may appear, at least to outsiders, rather fanciful and far-fetched. Yet, the mystic meanings thrown around the singularly lovely composition of *Matrimony* satisfy at least the poetic sense. The artist explains how in the frieze is seen the union of Christ with the Church—the heavenly architype of marriage—celebrated by a choir of angels. The predella presents a symbol from the Old Testament in Tobias, who, under divine guidance, obtains a companion for life. One side-border exemplifies the first institution of matrimony in Paradise; angels above, in embrace, are scattering flowers. On the opposite side an angel showers down thorns, and on the ground beneath lies the dead Saviour, signifying that marriage through suffering obtains its consecration. The painter ends with the closing prayer that "these seven Psalms which I have sounded on my harp may exhibit the teaching of the Church in its beauty and sublimity, and thus do honour to God, to whom alone are due glory and praise in time and in eternity. Amen."

Neither *The Seven Sacraments* as works of art, nor the printed notes thereto as treatises in theology, have been accepted by the world favourably. Even within the Roman Catholic Church they are deemed rather ultra; unfortunately the painter could not see when and where his art became an outrage on the common sense of mankind. His treatment of *Holy Communion* in these *Sacraments*, as well as in sundry other designs, is an instance of the way in which he pushed full far his sacerdotalism. He habitually departs from the treatment sanctioned by the great masters, from Giotto to Leonardo da Vinci; in place of a long table whereat all are seated is a small altar, before which the Apostles kneel; in lieu of a supper, the cloth is laid with only a plate and chalice, and instead of the breaking of bread among the disciples, Christ stands apart elevating a wafer. Now, all religious controversy aside, most minds will feel that, by thus substituting a fiction for a recorded fact, the subject is spoilt in point of art. And herein I cannot but recall a saying of Coleridge to the effect that he who begins by loving his Creed more than Christianity will end "by loving his Church more than truth."[7]

Between the Christian artist and the head of the Church grew, as might be expected, a bond of mutual respect and attachment. Overbeck and Pius IX. had much in common; they were as brothers in affliction; the age was unbelieving; they had fallen upon evil days; and each was sustained alike by unshaken faith in the Church. Concerning *The Stations*, the drawings of which are in the private rooms of the Vatican, the Pope showed the liveliest interest, and wrote a letter to the artist full of apostolic benedictions. He had also evinced his friendly regard by giving sittings for his portrait. Afterwards, in 1857, came the commission to paint, for the Quirinal Palace, the large tempera picture representing Christ miraculously escaping from the Jews, who, according to the Gospel of St. Luke, had "thrust him out of the city, and had led him to the brow of the hill whereon the city was built, that they might cast him down headlong." This astounding composition is the one step from the sublime to the ridiculous; it represents Christ with the right foot on the edge of a precipice, the left in the air on the heads of small angels: it was intended to symbolise the Pope's escape from Rome, and his subsequent return to the city; and further it expressly signified the triumph of the spiritual over the temporal power.[8] While the large and important work was in progress, Pius IX. paid a visit to the painter in his studio, an event to the honour of modern art comparable to the old stories touching Francis I. with Leonardo da Vinci and Philip IV. in the painting-room of Velazquez. This abortive miracle on canvas left on my mind, when seen in the studio, a very painful impression, and sound critics—Zahn and others— pronounce the subject as unpaintable, and the work most unfortunate. Overbeck had not the power possessed by the old masters of carrying the imagination into the age of miracle.

I have been at some pains to make the account here given of the painter's works exhaustive. My opportunities of observation have been favourable, and yet, especially as no complete biography of the artist has hitherto been published, some minor works may have escaped my notice. Here, in conclusion, may fitly come a few additions. *The Raising of Lazarus*, the exquisite drawing of which, now in the Düsseldorf Academy, has already received notice, was, in 1822, painted in oils. *The Death of St. Joseph*, before mentioned, was, in 1838, reproduced for the private chapel of the newly created Bishop of Algiers. Also worthy of mention are cartoons of *The Twelve Apostles* and of *The Four Evangelists*, for the Torlonia chapel at Castel Gondolfo; a design, *Christ teaching the Lord's Prayer*, for a window in the church of St. Katherine, Hamburg; sketches, including *The Coronation of the Virgin*, for a cathedral in Mexico; likewise drawings of the *Virtues*, also *Moses and the Daughters of Jethro*, the last engraved by Gruner, and then in England, belonging to Lord Hatfield. Also *The Vocation of St. John and St. James,* a pencil drawing in the possession of Baron Lotzbeck, Schloss Weihern, near Munich. This beautiful design has been chosen as one of the illustrations to this volume. Few masters have been so largely engraved as Overbeck; scarcely a picture or drawing of import exists that has not become thus widely diffused. By the artist's own hand are reproduced, on copper, *St. Philip Neri,* and a *Pilgrim.* In France were published the "Book of Hours," and "The Imitation of Christ," severally illustrated from designs by Overbeck. A pictorial art, chiefly reliant on form, and expressly intended for the teaching and saving of man, was fitly thus multiplied and disseminated.

Numerous portraits of Overbeck, by himself and friends, give a retrospective view of his character. Probably the earliest is a pencil drawing in the Vienna Academy by the Viennese painter, Johann Scheffer von Leonhardshoff; the date must be prior to 1810, and the age somewhere about twenty. The head is remarkable, almost abnormal; the outlook on the world is inquiring, querulous, and combative; the penetrative eyes seem in search after

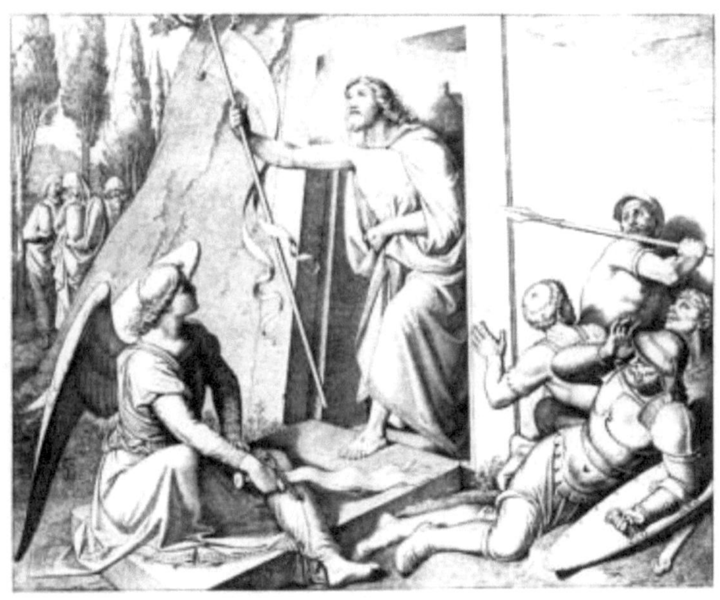

undiscovered truth; the pursed-up mouth is prepared for protest; the attenuated nose and contracted nostril betray austerity and acerbity; the whole aspect is that of nervous irritability. The spirit is still in unrest, having sought in vain for the ideal; and unsatisfied yearnings already settle into moody sentiment and melancholy. In these traits are clearly legible the painful perplexities and the severe conflicts of the painter's first period. And like mental states and bodily conditions are carried into the pencil likeness already mentioned, taken in Rome by Cornelius some three years later: for the moment the mind seems masked by a phlegmatic mass of German clay; whatever might be light-giving in the inward man appears clouded. This, as we have seen, was for the young painter a time of doubt and difficulty, and the face remains as yet unillumined. The next known portraits come at a long interval, and show marked changes, which tell of deep and not wholly blissful experiences. In

1837, Carl Küchler, who made a series of portraits of German painters living in Rome, took and engraved the likeness of Overbeck at
the age of forty-eight. The head is most striking and impressive; the
coronal regions, the reputed abode of the moral and religious faculties, rise in full development; the frontal lobes of the intellect, with
the adjacent territories of the imagination, bespeak the philosopher
and the poet, while the scant circuit of the posterior organs gives
slight sign of animal passion. The mien is that of a mediæval saint—
austere, devout; the eyes steadfastly gaze as on hidden mysteries,
yet shine with spiritual radiance; the brow, temple, and cheek are
those of the child, yet thinker; all the features have settled into meditative repose, gently shaded by melancholy. Overbeck, at this time
in close converse with Heaven, had given himself unreservedly to
Christian Art; hence this supremely ideal head. The portrait, contributed to the autograph collection of artists' heads in the Uffizi
Gallery, Florence, pleased neither the painter nor any one else, yet it
was carried out on the favourite doctrine of uniting the inward with
the outward man. The style is hard and dry, the character that of
starved asceticism; the expression is Jesuitical, and actual traits are
so exaggerated as barely to escape caricature. The artist was painted
by Carl Hoffmann, also, it is said, by Genelli and Ernst Deger. The
portraits in late life, whilst preserving personal identity, betray
somewhat painfully the inroads of age and ill health. Rudolf Lehmann made a faithful study in 1853; Adolf Grass, an inmate in the
house, painted in oils a portrait in 1865; and Professor Bendemann,
in 1867, prevailed upon the diffident old man to give a sitting. Two
years later death entered the house, and Friedrich Geselschap, a
friend and artist from Düsseldorf, came a few hours after the eyes
were closed, and made a full-size chalk drawing of the head as it
peacefully lay on the pillow. This faithful transcript, now on the
table before me, scarcely sustains the statement of some writers, that
the countenance after death assumed a glorified aspect; but, whether living or dying, peace, though not void of pain, is the pervading
expression.

Overbeck, after the goodly habit of the old masters, was fond of
introducing himself as a spectator in the sacred scenes he depicted,
and thus the above list of portraits is considerably extended. The
painter appears personally in *Christ's Entry into Jerusalem*; also, in

company with his friends Cornelius and Veit, he joins the general assembly of artists in *The Triumph of Religion*. Again, in *The Gospels* the devout painter is present at the Crucifixion, bent on his knees, the hands clasped, his eyes gazing on Christ upon the Cross. Overbeck was not thus the egotist or a man craving for glory, but merely the humblest of servants seeking some inconspicuous place among the followers of Christ, and desiring to be numbered with God's elect.

I have endeavoured, though perhaps very imperfectly, to lay before the reader a picture of Overbeck as the artist and the man, and now little remains save a few general conclusions. I have anxiously tried to ascertain the painter's mode of work, and the successive steps by which he matured his compositions. This inquiry has proved all the more difficult, because drawings in their early stages were persistently kept out of view. The artist had two studios, the one strictly private for quiet incubation apart; the other public, wherein only finished products were shown. The question is, how consummate designs such as *The Gospels* were elaborated. I find that Overbeck first revolved a subject in his thoughts until he had formed a distinct mental conception; this inward vision he would sometimes for months carry about with him, within the house and in his walks abroad. At last, when it had taken shape, he sketched out the idea with lead pencil on a small piece of paper; and, just in proportion as the first process had been tentative and slow, so was the final act swift and certain. In these supreme moments he had the power of throwing off his innermost thoughts without aids from the outer world: the lines flowed from his pencil rapidly when he had made up his mind what to do, and the forms once set down were seldom changed. The facility increased rather than lessened with years; thus we read, "At the age of seventy-two I create with undiminished freshness and pleasure." As soon as the first small sketch was complete, the usual method was followed of squaring out the surface with lines, in order to reproduce in charcoal, chalk, or sepia the design on the full scale required—often the size of life. For the important figures, for the heads, hands, and draperies, studies from the life were diligently made. Such drawings and cartoons have been and are greatly prized by connoisseurs; for example, *The Seven Years of Famine* was acquired by Sir Thomas Lawrence for his collection. The reader will understand how difficult it was for the painter to find assistants who could help in this directly personal work, in this concentration of individual thought; hence the prolonged time needed, extending, as we have seen, to periods of five or ten years. Separate studies of colour were also sometimes, if not always, made. The ultimate stage of painting upon canvas or wall was comparatively a mechanical process.

Furthermore, we have to consider and make allowance for certain technical notions of Overbeck and his school. The opinion upheld was that the idea or mental conception constituted the chief value of any art work, that outline or form was the direct language or vehicle of such idea, and that colour, light, shade, surface-texture, or realism, were subordinate, if not derogatory, elements. Thus it is that the works of the master cannot be judged by ordinary standards: hence likewise the drawings and cartoons are superior to the pictures.

Especially does Overbeck's colour stand in need of explanation or apology. In the first place we have to take into account how far the artist was bound to tradition; we have, for instance, to bear in mind that in painting *The Assumption*, he was enjoined by the Church to clothe the Madonna in white. Then comes the whole question of symbolism, or the inherent or accepted relation between colour and thought and feeling. Now, I think it probable that Overbeck sacrificed harmonies pleasing to the eye for the sake of arrangements that might inculcate doctrines or impress emotions. Certain it is that he looked on colour as something carnal: the example of the Venetian painters warned him against passionate excess, and so as a religious artist he felt it a duty to use sombre pigments, tertiary tints, and low, shadowy tones. Thus much needs explanation, yet it must always be cause for regret that Overbeck did not take for examples such masters of colour as Fra Angelico and Perugino, and thus gain the heavenly radiance begotten of religion.

The art of Overbeck will live by its merits despite its defects; it is vital and enduring in the three mental elements of thought, form, and composition. The last he matured and mastered with the certainty of a science and the beauty of an art. His compositions have the exactitude, and occasionally the complexity, of geometric problems, neither are they without the rhythm of a stanza, or the music of a song.

How much and in what manner the art of Overbeck was due to direct inspiration from heaven is not easy to determine. But, at all events, the modern master, like his forerunners in the spiritual school of Umbria, watched and waited, fasted, prayed, and painted. One who observed him closely testifies how, while making the drawings for *The Gospels* and *The Seven Sacraments*, he was penetrated with the life of Christ. From deep wells the infinite soul flowed into the finite mind, and the art conceived in the spirit of prayer issued as a renewed prayer to God.

The reader, I trust, has formed a judgment as to the three-fold relation in which Overbeck and his works stand to nature, to historic precedent, and lastly, to inward consciousness or individual character. We have seen that the notion prevalent in Rome, that the living model was wholly discarded, is inaccurate; bearing on this moot point may be here told an anecdote. It is related how one morning, when the artist was engaged on the Tasso frescoes, in the Villa Massimo, he had need of the life for a muscular arm, and so sallied forth into the neighbouring Piazza of the Lateran and made appeal to some men who were breaking stones on the road. One of the number, of amazing muscle, consented to sit, but, to the disgust of the purist painter, the man turned out to be a public executioner, who only took to stone breaking when slack of usual work. Another story is to the effect that, one day a fellow of terrific aspect entered the studio, declaring he was without food, and demanding engagement as a model. He turned out a villain, and so the aversion grew to coming in contact with common and unclean nature. Another reason assigned for the non-employment of models is the lack of sufficient strength to sustain protracted study from the life. Hence recourse to other methods: for instance, both mental and pencil notes were taken of casual figures and incidents in society or in the public streets. John Gibson, the sculptor, cultivated a like habit. Also a remarkable memory, of which much might be told, served as a storehouse of pictorial materials. It is recounted now on Sunday evenings, after the reception in the studio of fifty or a hundred guests, the meditative artist would recall and describe the visitors one by one, and after many years, and perhaps in a distant place, meeting some person, otherwise unknown, he would say, "I remember to have seen that face once in my painting-room." In like manner his memory was peopled with figures, whose acquaintance he had made only in pictures: thus, when he came to paint *The Assumption* for Cologne Cathedral, he had recourse to the mental vision of the Madonna, derived from an old Sienese panel, and, when charged with the plagiarism, he replied: "The figure realises my idea, and I do not see why I should search further." Thus, however, it came to pass that he borrowed more and more from others, just in proportion as he took less from nature. But in coming to a fair judgment, we have to remember that the accidents in nature, and the grosser materialism in man, were foreign to this super-sensuous art, the aim being to reach the hidden meaning and the inner life. Hence the favourite practice of placing and posing in the painting-room some well-chosen figure which was quietly looked at, carefully considered, and taken in; thus the irrelevant elements were eliminated, and only the essential truths assimilated. This was for Overbeck the saving study of nature: he made extracts and essences, elaborated generic types, and thus his art became supreme in beauty. However, the beautiful is not always new, neither is the new always beautiful.

The painter's relation to the historic schools of Christian Art has been so fully stated, that little more remains to be said. The old masters were studied much in the same way as nature: their spirit was inhaled, and just as John Gibson was accustomed to ask, What would the Greeks have done? so Overbeck put himself in the place of the early Italian painters, and desired that his pencil might be guided by their spirit. Like Raphael, what he borrowed he made his own, and often added an aspect and a grace peculiar to himself. A gallery of pictures was for him what a well-stored library is to a literary student, who takes from the shelves the author best supplying the intellectual food needed. The method is not new or strange: Bacon teaches how the moderns inherit the wisdom of the ancients, and surely if for art, as for learning, there be advancement in store, old pictures, like old books, must give up the treasure of a life beyond life. Overbeck in the past sought not for the dead, but for the living and enduring.

Given a painter's genius and surroundings, his art usually follows under the law of cause and effect. Overbeck's pictures, as those of others, yield under analysis as their component parts, nature plus tradition, plus individual self. As to the individual man, we have found Overbeck the poet and philosopher, the mystic, somewhat the sentimentalist, and, above all, the devout Catholic. The character is singularly interesting, and the products are unusually complex. He had forerunners and many imitators, yet he stands alone, and were his pencil lost, a blank would be felt in the realm of art. His genius was denied grandeur: he did not rise to the epic, and scarcely expanded into the dramatic; his path was comparatively narrow; his kingdom remained small, yet where he stands is hallowed ground; his art is musical, altogether lyrical, yet toned with pathos, as if the lamentations of The Holy Women at the Sepulchre mingled with the angel-voices of The Nativity. The man and his work are among the most striking and unaccustomed phenomena of the century, and so far as his art is true to God, humanity, and nature, it must endure. His own assurance is left on record: he held that knowledge and doing are of value only so far as they ennoble humanity, and lead to that which is eternal. He believed in the dependence of art on personal character, on elevation of mind and purity of motive. The noblest destiny of the race was ceaselessly before him, and he looked to Christian Art as the means of showing to the world the everlasting truth, and of raising the reality of life to the ideal. In conclusion, I think it not too much to claim Overbeck as the most perfect example, in our time, of the Christian Artist.

The pecuniary rewards of the painter were in no fair proportion to his talents or his industry. His labour, as we have seen, was primarily for the honour of art and religion, and his protracted modes of study, as well as the esoteric character of his compositions, were little likely to meet with adequate return. Overbeck never realised large sums; his prices measured by present standards were ridiculously low, and even when overcrowded with commissions, he is known to have fallen short of ready cash. Happily, after early struggles, he became relieved from pressing anxieties, yet he remained comparatively poor.

Overbeck's influence, the example of his life, the principles of his art, extended far and wide throughout Europe. In France, the German master won the reverence of the Christian artist Flandrin. In England, Pugin held him up to students as a bright example. In Vienna and Prague, Joseph Führich, as a disciple, worked diligently. In Munich, Heinrich Hess, and in Spires, Johann Schraudolph, painted extended series of frescoes allied to the same Christian school. In Düsseldorf like traditions live:—Deger, Ittenbach, Carl and Andreas Müller studied in Rome, and their frescoes in the Rhine chapel at Remagen were inspired by Overbeck. And specially does the mantle of the revered painter rest on his friend Eduard Steinle; important works at Strasbourg, Cologne, Frankfort, Münster, Klein-Heubach, and Reineck, respond to the spirit of the great artist who, dead, yet speaks.

Brief is the narrative of the approaching end. The infirmities of age scarcely abated the ardent pursuit of an art dear as life itself. Overbeck had suffered from an affection of the eyes, and his later drawings, notwithstanding partial panegyrists, betray a faltering hand, together with some incoherence in thought, or, at least, in the relation of the parts to the whole. For some time, in fact, vitality had been ebbing from his work. The summer of 1869 found him in his favourite retreat of Rocca di Papa, and we are told he was "still busily creating." His country dwelling stood among beauties which, in illness as in health, came with healing power. From this sylvan quietude the aged painter, in June, wrote to his dear friend, Director Steinle, a letter abounding in love and aspiration; he dwells on the serenity of the Italian sky, on the splendour of the landscape stretching before his eye into the far distance; with characteristic modesty he laments that even in old age he is not sufficiently advanced for the great task set before him, and desires without intermission to turn to good account the time still left; and then he counsels his "Brother in Christ" to direct the mind steadfastly towards the glorious olden days which point to the blessed goal.

Overbeck, on his return to Rome in the autumn of 1869, resumed his accustomed order of life. One who knew him well in later years relates that he was to be found in his studio in the early morning, that, after a short interval at noon, he resumed work till stopped by the darkness of evening, and that, such was the wealth of material stored in the mind, that he went on inventing without aid from usual outward appliances. He still sought utmost tranquillity, and any intrusion on the hours of study became extremely painful to him. Latterly he had been engaged on a small composition of *The Last Judgment*; also he was occupied on designs illustrative of human life—a series which had advanced as far as the *Return from Church of the Wedding Party*. Such were the congenial avocations when, on the fourteenth day after the return home, he was seized with a severe cold on the chest. Yet the symptoms so far yielded to medical treatment that in eight days the danger had passed. Suddenly, however, ensued a total failure of power, yet for the most part the mind remained unclouded. A day or two before death he asked for a piece of charcoal, and added a few touches to a design on which lately he had been working; and at times, when apparently unconscious, he would look upwards, raise and move his hand as if in the act of drawing. He prayed almost without ceasing, was grateful for each kindness, and with dying lips had a loving and comforting word for everyone. The last sinking came in quietness; sustained by the consolations of religion he fell asleep towards six o'clock in the evening of Friday, the 12th of November, in the eightieth year of his age. He lay as he had lived—in peace; and near his bed was placed the drawing on which he had lately worked, also the small cartoon of *The Last Judgment*.

The next day, according to the painter's wish, the body was taken by the hands of his brother artists to San Bernardo, the little parish church near his house, where he worshipped, and where he is still remembered. An eye-witness writes from Rome to Lübeck, on the 18th of November: "I have just come from the burial of our great fellow-countryman. Amid universal grief the funeral mass took place this morning. The mournful ceremony was performed by a German bishop assisted by Cistercian monks; many artists and German students were present, and joined in psalms composed by the Abbé Liszt. The whole function was most solemn, as if the pious spirit of the departed had entered the whole assembly. Around the bier were gathered Protestants as well as Roman Catholics; the coffin bore the many orders which the artist had received, but was never seen to wear; and at the feet lay the crown of laurels which his Roman brethren reverently offered to their acknowledged chief." The body lies in the chapel of St. Francis of Assisi, within the church of San Bernardo. The resting-place is marked by a white marble cross, let into the wall, bearing the inscription "Joannes Fridericus Overbeck—In Pace."

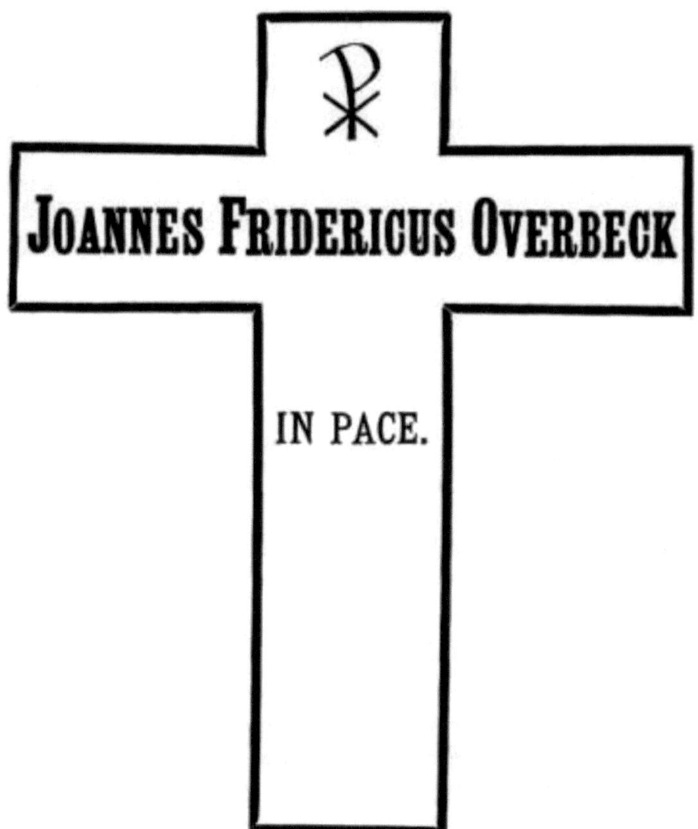

The Resting-place of Overbeck in the Church of San Bernardo,
Rome, is
marked by a Cross of white marble bordered with black, and bearing
an inscription as above.

FOOTNOTES:

[1] See 'Lübeckische Blätter,' from 1839 to 1869, for sundry notices concerning this picture and other works. The *Pietà* is in oil on canvas, 10 feet wide and nearly as high; the top is arched; it is photographed. The pigments are in usual sound condition. A small picture accompanied this *Pietà*. It had been intended as a present to the brother, Judge Christian Gerhard Overbeck, but his death, in 1846, preventing the fulfilment of the purpose, it was sent to Lübeck as a gift to his son, the artist's nephew, Doctor and Senator Christian Theodore Overbeck, who died 1880. The representatives in Lübeck of this nephew are said to be in possession of sundry memorials of the illustrious uncle. Here in Lübeck I may mention a *Madonna and Child*, a circular composition 3 feet 2 inches in diameter, with the painter's monogram and the date 1853. The picture is a gem, exquisite for purity, tenderness, and beauty. Another *Madonna and Child* is in the Thorwaldsen Museum, Copenhagen.

[2] *The Incredulity of St. Thomas* is 10 feet high by 5 feet wide. It bears the painter's monogram and the date 1851. The figures are life-size. The picture is in perfect preservation. The pigments, as usual, lie thin, showing through the rough tissues of the Roman canvas.

[3] See 'Geschichte der neuen Deutschen Kunst, von Ernst Förster.' Leipzig, Weigel, 1863.

[4] *The Assumption of the Virgin* is in oil on canvas; height about 18 feet, width 9 feet. Figures nearly life-size. The scale is rather small for the magnitude of the architectural surroundings. The tone is that of an old picture, low and solemn. No positive colours are admitted. The pigments remain intact, without crack, blister, or change of colour. The picture was the joint gift of the Düsseldorf Kunst-Verein and the Cologne Cathedral Chapter. The price paid was equal to about £1000 sterling. The cartoon was exhibited in 1876 in the National Gallery, Berlin.

[5] The cartoons of the *Via Crucis* were, in September 1880, in the Villa Germania, near Biebrich. They are in chalk or charcoal in outline on grey ground, tinted with sepia. Height, 1 foot 9 inches; breadth, 1 foot 5 inches. The water-colour drawings of the same series were, in January, 1878, in the Camera di Udienza of the Vati-

can. Height, 2 feet 6 inches; width, 1 foot 8 inches; mounted on white, and massively framed. The walls and accessories of the Pope's apartment are of a crude colour and in bad taste. The feeble execution of these cartoons and water-colour drawings betrays advancing age and declining power.

[6] The cartoons of *The Seven Sacraments*, after a labour of some eight years, were finished in 1861, and received high encomiums when exhibited in Brussels. They remained with Overbeck at the time of his death, together with many other artistic properties, the accumulation of a life. Some of these treasures have been sold by the family who entered into possession. The cartoons were offered for sale, but are still without a purchaser. Small tempera drawings of *The Seven Sacraments* were bought for the National Gallery, Berlin, in 1878. They are on canvas: measurement, 1 foot 8 inches by 1 foot 3 inches. These reductions were entrusted to scholars; the execution is poor; the master is responsible chiefly for revision. The pigments used vary; some are in warm sepia, others in cooler tones, and one, *Penance*, is fully coloured. The results technically are far from satisfactory. These *Sacraments*, including the predellas, friezes, and side borders, have been photographed in large and smaller sizes by Albert, Munich, and from the photographs August Gaber executed woodcuts, published with explanatory text penned by Overbeck. This text was also published as a separate pamphlet: Dresden, August Gaber; London, Dulau and Co. The hope above expressed that the cartoons might be further carried out was never realised.

[7] I was informed, in October, 1881, by August Gaber, that the wood engravings made by him of *The Seven Sacraments* had proved a financial failure, and that he had in the undertaking lost his all. The Bible of Schnorr, also rendered on wood by him, had, on the contrary succeeded. The reason assigned why the public did not care for *The Seven Sacraments* was, that the treatment is too strongly Catholic; and this can hardly be a prejudiced judgment, because it was pronounced by Herr Gaber, himself a Catholic.

[8] The picture is in tempera on canvas, and was put up on the ceiling of Pio Nono's sitting room in the Quirinal Palace. But when the King of Italy took possession, a new canvas with cupids and

putti was stretched over it, and the Pope's sitting room is now turned into Prince Humbert's bedroom. This brutality might almost justify the good painter in his belief that Satan is now let loose upon earth. Yet the plea has not without reason been urged that the picture is a deliberate attack on the King's temporal power. The original cartoon was, in 1876, exhibited in the National Gallery, Berlin, and the same subject the artist repeated in an oil picture (10 feet by 8 feet), now in the Antwerp Museum. Overbeck had been made a "Membre effectif" of the Antwerp Academy in 1863, and the commission for this *replica* followed thereon. I am told on authority that in Antwerp "the work is considered very mediocre."